Teetering on the Brink

Teetering on the Brink

Best Wishes,

Gary O. Weibye

Gary Weibye

ISBN 1-59109-584-0

Teetering on the Brink

Table of Contents

Introduction

The stories and sketches presented here somehow resemble the truth. Some of the characters are composites, some are thinly-disguised replicas, and some never personally existed but were needed to tell about the others. They have the qualities and foibles of neighbors, friends, and strangers I have encountered while living on the rim of what tourists are instructed to call "The Grand Canyon of the Ozarks."

We are "rim folk," if you will: "seasoned" people, teetering on the brink—contemplating The View, the climb behind us, and the plunge ahead. We spend whole mornings in pink clouds where, by rights, choirs should be singing! We live in almost ridiculous beauty, and the place shapes us. We think the thoughts human beings stumble upon when an abyss is at their feet, whether the abyss is an actual canyon or a stage of life, and we smile.

We are not immune to what the tourists come here to see. Many of us are tourists who just *stayed*—who are retired now, and living in what passers-through call "scenery." We are the lucky ones, the decisive ones, perhaps the wise ones. We often stop, and drop our endeavors at our feet, and stand stupified once again, and try to absorb the wonder, and fumble for words or poems or songs or prayers. We do not scoff at the "window shoppers" in the scenic overlooks. We are the window shoppers who fell through the window.

The events depicted here are scrambled, exaggerated, compressed, or invented—the names changed, the details muddled—to get at the essence of the place. And in the end, this is about a place, and the place is real. Call it autobiographical fiction.

Gary Weibye

To Wifey, for rescuing me and taking me away into the hills.

Unloading Claude

One of the first things that needed work when I retired and moved off into the hills was my ability to take it easy, disengage, relax, slow down. Failure at retirement was not going to be an option. Wifey and I re-located, spectacularly! We left behind a seething city with world-class traffic where for years we had flailed away day and night in thankless efforts (she, a nurse; I, a teacher), and our new life was going to be spent in a county where there was not one traffic light, even a yellow caution flasher at a fire station, and where people lived amid astonishing natural beauty—utterly distracting scenery. Without deadlines. It would be a challenge, because we considered ourselves to be two complicated people popping abruptly into an uncomplicated world.

We were both refreshingly naive about retirement, old age, living in the country, and "standing down."

Where I had worked, a bell would ring and two thousand kids would run over my arches on their way to fist fights, dope deals, love trysts, parole officer appointments, math class, body-piercing sessions, and cheerleader practice. Where Wifey worked, The Powers would try to stick her with eighteen critical care patients for the night shift. We burnt out and went away.

Claude Benson found us a couple of weeks after we took up residence in the hills. He saw activity at our place, and his curiosity got him, and he pulled his bright and shiny SUV into our driveway. We were happy to have a new friend, made him welcome, and began getting to know him, exchanging vital statistics and background information, rapid-fire, as was our habit: all executed during simultaneous move-in and crank-up activities. We told him too much, and he opened up pretty well, too—for a retired IRS tax accountant. I liked him: he wore great hats. And instead of saying good-bye, he glanced at his snazzy wristwatch and said, "Keep records," then started his car and left. Clever.

Two weeks into this new life, we were still operating at 100 mph.: cleaning, painting, unpacking, and rearranging—planning, repairing, building, and culling—adjusting, arguing, re-thinking, and collapsing. Claude Benson learned that he was going to talk to someone who was pounding nails, caulking windows, gasping over the natural beauty, painting shutters, or hanging out a wash—if he wanted to talk to us at all. We had not yet learned to drop everything and socialize. Perhaps we could have been interpreted as rude.

∿

"You know what?" he said on his second visit, "You guys have got to learn to relax. You're retired now. There's no big emergency."

"What ever do you mean?" I asked, frantically juggling several tools.

"I mean you guys are still wired for the city. You're in Work Mode. Chill out." And then he said, "Eeeasy, Eeeeasy!"—which we found to be cute that first time.

His visits were short, and that was okay with us. We had a frantic schedule going.

Two days after his second visit, we received a "Thank You" note from our new friend. He thanked us for talking to him and listening to him. He signed with, "Eeeasy...! And keep records."

And so we tried. He was right: we had to ease up. And we thought we were doing a pretty good job when we were only doing two things at once. We resolved to get it down to one thing. We deliberately slowed down, for Claude. In traffic, the steep hills helped us focus: the sheer terror of the dive into the village, the hairpin turns, the plummeting, the free-fall, the howling tires. I learned to look directly at the person I was talking to rather than survey the entire landscape, my back to a wall: school behavior. Wifey quit taking vital signs (when her machine broke). We made progress. I insist.

But Claude still kept after us. "Slow down. Just get organized. You've got a chance to put chaos out of your life here. Easy...eeeasy!" Just a little drop-in session, quick and clean. The sparkling SUV became a familiar sight.

And another "Thank you" arrived. This time it thanked us for not being afraid.

"What the hell does that mean?" I said to Wifey.

"Former IRS man. Probably spooks some people."

"Could be."

At Claude's written invitation, we visited him at his place out on a nearby "point" of land that had an even more spectacular view than we had. Claude greeted us as we pulled in, looking at his watch and waving. We were on time.

It was a neat, impressive-looking home, completely fenced, tastefully painted, and trimmed with native rock. And we began to notice things. Claude was bald, completely, and always wore pressed blue jeans, now that we thought about it, and ironed shirts, immaculate boots. His SUV was always clean, as if washed daily: we had never seen it otherwise. His house and yard were mathematically proportioned, pleasing to the eye, balanced. I didn't even want to look into his garage. I could only imagine. We had had a garage in the city, and it was a nightmare that could never admit an actual car into its cluttered confines. His flower beds were perfect. We had to check to see if the flowers were even real. All plants had tags or labels. It went on like that when we got inside the house.

We took off our shoes at the door—without coaching. Somehow, it just seemed right. Claude gave us a tour of the parts of the house he shared with guests. Wifey and I, as always, had two completely different experiences, we noted later. I noticed his meditation schedule and his exercise schedule, both timed, posted on a bulletin board. I noticed that his furniture was modern and under-stuffed and stationary. (Me, I need a rocker somewhere) There was no TV, but there was a computer room that looked like the cockpit of a 747, and every drawer anywhere had an inventory list stuck to it. Wifey noticed that his pantry was alphabetized and that each item had a date label—and as back-up, on the inside of the pantry door there was an IN/OUT check list, dated also. She glanced out a window and saw trash cans of various colors, marked A, B, C, D, and E and lined up beside an out-building. Something we both noticed was the Mission Statement, framed and hung on the wall of the great room

And then Claude handed us each a printed menu. We were having a snack, and the menu listed our options: fruits and vegetables, mainly, raw. A choice of drinks . There was no Mrs. Benson at the moment: out of town. But then, we were all out-of-town, weren't we? Nevertheless, our lunch was perfect: china, silver, place mats, napkins in napkin rings, the whole nine yards. Wifey and I had to search our memory banks to know what the hell to do, how to behave. I could sense that Wifey wanted out as badly as I did.

"I thought you might profit from seeing this," said Claude, handing us each a stapled, five-page document. "It could help you to relax a little. You both seem nervous, even now, and you have been gone from that city for weeks!" It was entitled *Relaxation Through Organization*

A bell chimed in the kitchen area, and Claude arose and went over and took something out of the freezer. He looked at his watch, fiddled with a few settings, then returned to the table.

I did a quick skim of the document, and I realized that we were in trouble. Under the table Wifey's foot went to work. In all future at-table sessions, I would be kicked black and blue when urgent communication was necessary. As usual, Wifey was right. The document was a list of a hundred and fifty things we could do at our house to organize things, and therefore deliver ourselves from worry and hurry, and I had several wisecracks that I would have offered if not for the merciless kicking. The last page was a book list: self help, organization, Yoga, etc.

We learned a lot that day. Claude wore boxers, to get right to it, and they were ironed: had sharp creases that could cut your fingers. He did not drink or smoke. He slept in blindfolds and earplugs, he told us for some reason, and he did not watch television. He went to bed at eleven p.m. and he arose at 6:30 a.m. daily, 365 days a year; he did not eat meat, including poultry; he shaved every morning and every evening, including his head; all of his lights were on timers, some were on motion detectors; all of his bulbs were those long-life, ecological jobs; he changed all of his smoke alarm batteries in Spring and Fall when Daylight Savings Time flip-flopped; he changed the oil in his car every 3000 miles, carried belts and hoses at all times, had an on-board compressor and battery charger in his SUV; in winter he had Kitty Litter for traction, blankets for warmth, flares for emergencies, trail mix, a shovel, tool kit, cellular phone. All of this supposedly relaxed him. The guy just drove me nuts.

We fled as soon as we could gracefully get out of there. He insisted there was no hurry, but he looked at his watch, too. I had a slight limp, because of my attempts at the table to comment on some of the repartee. Wifey must have had a sore foot, too.

At the car (our pick-up), he could not conceal his disenchantment with the dust on the outside and the chaos on the inside. "They have a car wash down in the town, you know," he commented, marking his territory in the dust on the hood of the vehicle. Then he waved and yelled, "Keep records," as we pulled out.

On the way home, I read aloud from Claude's document as Wifey drove. "Number One, make lists of things to do tomorrow, along with approximate times; Number Two, make a list of all raw materials needed for the month's projects, to avoid unnecessary trips to town; Number Three, groom yourself daily: grooming is the first thing to go in rural life; Number Four...Wait a minute! Who the hell does this clown think he is?"

"You shouldn't have invited him over," said Wifey.

"I think it was you who invited him..."

"Well, you have no manners. Maybe it was."

Claude was going to be my fault now.

ॐ

"Number Four," I read from Claude's list that evening while watching TV, massaging my leg, and eating dinner, "the tools in your garage can be organized alphabetically, in a left-to-right configuration, or a top-to-bottom motif. Colored tape can also be used...

"Oh, My God. We don't even have a garage yet!" I zoomed ahead. "Number Thirty-Seven, organize the contents of your refrigerator according to Tupperware size and color. Stick-on labels are optional...Number eighty-eight, the following numbers should be on your speed dial...

"Who the hell is this guy? Martha Stewart?"

The "Thank You" note we received the next day was for a previous visit, but the next one was for our visiting him. "Thank you ever so much for visiting me this afternoon. I have some things I would like to discuss with you, at your convenience. I will call you. Claude."

"Oh, My God," said Wifey. It was her turn.

"Keep the thought," I said, "Keep the thought."

But why, oh why, was he in our lives? What kind of mess were we in here? This guy lived a mile from us, and we were not going away, and neither was he, probably. What had we gotten ourselves into? And what did he want to "discuss" now?

Trying to make the best of it, I went through his whole list. I knew that he was right about having a system for filing all receipts, checks, contracts, warranties, guarantees, insurance policies, mortgages, transcripts, diplomas, deeds, easements, mineral and water rights, registrations, licenses, divorce papers, marriage licenses, owner's manuals, stocks and bonds and mutual funds, yada yada yada. All that crap was in our house somewhere. But I couldn't get into his closet organizers, his dated underwear and socks, his little holsters for his credit cards, driver's license, passport, Social Security card, folding money—or his recommended hardware: beeper, cell phone, compass, global positioning unit, etc. I wouldn't live long enough to do all that. And I refused to consider a formal Action Plan. I, for one, did not want to punch a clock in my old age, in my own house.

Claude checked us several times by phone: were we looking at the list? Were we considering all of it? Did we realize that winter was coming? Had we slowed down, meditated, gotten an exercise program going, set up a hundred schedules for everything from manicures to defecation? And could he please have a Progress Report? Wifey was courteous on the phone for a minute or two and then shuttled it over to me. He talked cheerily, invasively, in a structured manner, as if he were reading from a list. "You'll want to consider an alarm system. I have some recommendations..." And just before we hung up, he said, "Keep records!"

❧

"You've got to unload this guy," said Wifey. "He's a kook."

"Me? *I've* got to unload him?"

"He's *your* friend."

"I couldn't do that, " I said. "I am simply not that kind of man."

"Yes you are," said Wifey.

"But..." I countered cleverly.

"You had better be."

I dreaded his next drop-in. I wanted to take a trip, go back to the city for some privacy, get the hell outa Dodge! I was not relaxing now: I was sitting around worrying, spooked, distressed.

❧

"You guys still look nervous," Claude said on his next visit. "You have the look of panic—you look a little frantic. Eeeasy, eeeasy! What can I do to help you relax? Are you guys meditating yet? You're overdue." He looked at his watch.

"Claude, we're fine," Wifey told him.

We all stepped around back, and The View grabbed us for a

while, and we were all silent. It was all the meditation I needed. It lasted a couple of minutes. There was a pink cloud in the valley—lost.

"I see you're marking off ground for your new garage. Would you like a list of local contractors, or are you going to build it yourself?"

"We have found someone," I said.

"What?" said Claude, stepping back and eyeing us with a hurt, surprised look. "You have contracted?"

"Yeah."

"Well, did you take bids?"

"Yeah. Three. Picked one, and we'll start next week."

"Signed papers? Put money down?"

"Yep. And we are keeping records."

Claude looked perplexed. I could sense his mind racing ahead, out to the sides, all around the problem. His eyes darted everywhere. He took off his little hat and crunched it in his fist. Then he looked off into the view.

"You need a profile of all those contractors, really; and you need to know about each of the workers; and the raw materials need to be checked over..."

"Well, we did some of that..."

"But you haven't the resources. You need more than the county's eleven Yellow Pages. You need to do some digging. You need a computer. I could get you some listings. Who is doing the cement? What mixture? Are they dependable? Are they going to build the trusses or order them from a manufacturer? Better check that out. Remove some of the worry."

I stepped a few feet away from Wifey, because I knew I was going to do something stupid. "Maybe we could get an FBI background check of everything. The IRS might have some papers on them, too." Wifey could not get to me with her foot. "Or maybe the Secret Service or the CIA. I'd hate to just jump in there..." And I meant that in the best possible way. "The NSA, the BBB, hell, maybe the PTA! The SPCA and the NAACP might need to be consulted."

❦

Claude did not say, "Eeeasy, eeeasy!" He said, "Never mind," very coldly, moving briskly out of the back yard. "I did not mean to interfere. I was simply trying to make things easier and less stressful."

"It's okay, Claude," said Wifey.

"No, I need to mind my own business. I'll make a note of it. I do think it would be good to leave a little room for a generator in that garage, though. You need gas, electric, solar, wood, and a back-up, gasoline-operated generator up here, you know. And you'll need a maintenance schedule for each system." He was making his way to the front, stepping over the debris of our latest project, moving fast. "Winter will come. You will see."

We both followed, but Claude was moving. "Now, don't go away mad, Claude. You have given us some useful stuff. Lots of it, really. I was just joking." See there, I was apologetic, almost contrite, half-way sincere.

"Wait! I'm baking you some bread. I have jams; I have jellies..." said Wifey, fading, tentatively raising her hand, then withdrawing it.

"Excellent," he said. "Keep records! See you later." And he left, in a real snit, I'd say.

"This is your fault, too," said Wifey, but she could not hide her relief.

"I know."

I was sure I had stiff-armed Claude pretty good, and I would not have been surprised if he decided never to return. I could have lived with it if he had come over and told me off, or, like a parent back at school, called me names and cussed me out. If weeks or months had passed with no contact at all, I would have expected it. I had taken a good shot at unloading Claude.

But the next day Claude's immaculate SUV was there in our driveway. He was in a terrible hurry, but he had time to drop off a few things: lumber prices in the area, concrete prices, steel prices, sheeting and insulation prices, roofing prices—organized by alpha, by distance from our house, and by price—with brand names and *Consumer Reports* evaluations and recommendations. His statistics showed that our contractor would be at least the second choice, and therefore good. He even had a list of local saw mills, in case we wanted to go with ungraded native lumber.

He stopped abruptly, looked at his watch, hit a small button on it. "Really, you need to consider some really aggressive relaxation. And you and your wife could get into competitive speed meditating. Think about it."

Then he left in a hurry, betraying no sign of bitterness. It took me until ten at night to calm down and realize what all had been put into my hands.

❧

Then he was gone. It broke off, right there. Claude was apparently over: unloaded. Glutton for punishment, I gave him a call, and I told his answering machine that I was just checking in to see what was shakin'. But I felt a great deal of relief. There was no reply.

❧

Much of what Claude had shared with us was indeed useful—in fact, we considered a lot of it. There were some real common sense nuggets. We did manage to slow down, but I discovered that I was most relaxed when I was busy, when I had purpose, when I was, in fact, a little weary. I was needed, I was seeing progress, I was being rewarded with accomplishment. A little bourbon at sunset helped, too. I was fine. You know: happy. Wifey got hooked up with some local ladies, and she eased up a little, too. We got it going: bliss.

❧

One day Claude's SUV was in the driveway once again. It was dirty—no delicate way of saying it: it was filthy. You could write your name on it in the dust. It looked as neglected as my little truck. I was convinced immediately that Claude was dead, or that he had sold his car.

A lady about our age got out of the SUV and looked at our house as if a little confused. She looked at a clipboard she was carrying, shook her head, and tentatively approached the house. Our half-built garage was a mess; our vehicles were filthy and parked at strange angles; our house looked terrible—half-painted, somewhat scaffolded, ugly. It always looked ugly. She came to the front door anyway.

"Hello there. I am Claude's wife. I believe you know Claude Benson?"

"Sure," said Wifey. "Come on in."

Mrs. Benson was dressed modestly in a jogging outfit, somewhat crinkly, and her hair was a frightful mess. Wifey liked her right away, and so did I. But she had news for us, and after the usual, "My-oh-my-but-you-do-have-a-view-don't-you?" routine, we hunkered down over cookies and drinks and got to the business of Claude.

"I found you through your jacket in Claude's files. I thought I had better fill you in."

"Wait a minute. Claude has a file on us?" Right away, I didn't like that!

"On everybody," said Mrs. Benson. "Everybody up here. It will take me a week to get rid of them. Claude won't be needing them anymore."

"What's the deal?" said Wifey.

"Claude is in a private sanitarium in another state—never mind where. He sorta crashed and burned, if I can get informal. You didn't notice how he was living?"

"We noticed," I said. "He was...a detail man."

The lady looked at me like I was mocking her, feigning stupidity, deliberately baiting her. I had seen the look when I was deliberately baiting the mothers of problem children back at school. But then she realized that I was really trying to minimize Claude's affliction, understating things.

"Detail man? It was a sickness. It drove me out of the house and kept everyone else away! We came out here from fast lane city life, and he got obsessed with slowing down and smelling the flowers—to the point where just meeting the tight schedule of his so-called relaxation measures consumed all of his time. The house is so full of gadgets that just maintaining their bulbs and transistors and batteries and fuses and all that crap ate up his life. He finally snapped."

"My God," said Wifey, one more time.

"How did that look?" I asked.

Again, I got a strange look. "How did that look? It looked like crap! That's how it looked! What do you mean, how did it look?"

"I mean, how did it finally manifest itself? What happened? When he snapped, I mean."

"He shut down. He just quit, sat staring for God knows how long. I found him there, half starved, staring out at the mountains, the house raging on automatically all around him. His watch had even stopped. I wasn't even supposed to be there, but something told me...You didn't notice the ambulance?"

"Ambulance. Not really. That's not unusual." (The county ambulance barn was two miles away.)

"Well, we knew it was coming. Three years ago we had an intervention. See, he gets all these systems going, and he develops a consciousness for each system, and he runs himself ragged trying to keep up. He worried about everything. He actually worried about osmosis, photosynthesis, erosion, the carbon cycle—things going on all around you all the time. Then he pulled in other people, like you, I suppose, and worried about everything of theirs! A shrink came up with this big intervention: we pulled him back from all of it. But then we got out here, where I thought it would be okay, and he just went loony on me. Finally, he just shorted out and sat there like one of his gadgets with the power turned off."

"My Lord, I hope nothing I said caused any of this," I said.

"Probably not. No, he was just willing to take on all of your potential worries, re-structure your lives, forcibly calm you down, if necessary, and adjust your speed...Look, it was what he did. He did that to me, to his family, to everybody, and from the looks of his files, he had a good start on the whole neighborhood!"

She broke up a little at that point. Claude was, after all, her husband. "He's getting help now," she said. "It could have been worse, according to the shrinks."

I couldn't imagine. Mrs. Benson was headed for the front door, but I had to ask, "How could it have been worse?"

"This is the Bible Belt," she said. "Can you imagine what it would have been like if one of these folks had got him thinking about God?"

I couldn't imagine that, either. We let her go at that point, not even curious about how complicated it could have been. My mind was having a backlash, and it was time for a minor sip of bourbon and a long gaze into The View. But it was true, I suppose: Claude would have tried to take over for God.

Wifey and I decided that we were relatively uncomplicated people after all, but that we were not going to worry about it. Much.

We do think about Claude, once a year, at tax time. We're not perfect, but we keep records.

A Secret Room

The house was fatally, perpetually, and hopelessly unsatisfactory. From the moment we saw it and knew that we had to have it, the house was unacceptable: ugly, not unlike a double-wide trailer house, reeking of lowliness and cheapness. The authors of "location, location, location" cut their real estate teeth right there in the front yard. The realtor's sign out front was the classiest thing visible from the curb. What we bought was The View. For if you shut your eyes to the front of the house and the way it squatted there on the hillside, and if you just felt your way around back, you found yourself looking at a magnificent vista: a forty-mile view of a beautiful Ozark valley. Absolutely spectacular.

In those first few months, I was inside every wall and ceiling and floor of that structure with tools foreign to my hands. I replaced windows and doors, woodwork and paint, paneling and carpeting. Everything inside and out was the wrong size or shape or color. I abandoned my English teacher propensities and became a plumber, an electrician, a carpenter, a mason, a painter, a demolitions man. A dilettante, of course. We had tradesmen come and install a staircase and build a garage (as I studied them and learned). I added decking, landscaping, shrubbery, with Wifey calling the shots. We worked with timbers and stone and cement.

We were retired after long careers. This pageant of drudgery was our "rest" as we entered Seniorhood.

❧

"This was the bootlegger's house, you know," one of

the workers told us as the garage went up. "He was the best bootlegger in the county. Operated here for years, and never got caught." The guy's voice and demeanor reeked of admiration for that lawbreaker. He looked around at details of the walls and at the deck from which The View was most glorious.

"Bootlegger, huh?" I said, probing for more.

"Oh, yeah. You'd drive right through where this garage is now and into the rec room—which was his garage at the time." And he walked me through the place. "These windows were the double doors of that garage back then, and you'd just drive in, place your order, then back out and take off with your booze."

The house was located in a dry county in the Bible Belt, on top of a mountain, along a paved highway, and it was locally famous. The bootlegger did not run a still and create moonshine; he simply bought great stashes of beer and wine and hard liquor out of county and off mountain, and transported it to our place, and sold it to the locals. And the sheriff did not care, apparently. Not the "old" sheriff. It was a cottage industry, a tradition, a necessity, and a legend: a vital organ of the county.

"These stairs weren't here," the worker said, "and this sidewalk—see the way it slopes?—this was the ramp into the garage." I could see it perfectly, now that this worker explained it. "You didn't even have to get out of your car: he'd be there at your window like a car hop. Best damned bootlegger in the county."

"Seems like somebody would turn him in," I ventured.

"Somebody did—often. The Baptists and the good ladies of the county, the library folks, all the busybodies—they did that a lot. But he was never caught."

"The sheriff?"

"Had one sheriff that did business here, but they elected a new one, and he raided this place over and over again, but never caught him with nothin'. Best damned bootlegger ever was."

Then the worker drifted off into The View, as most visitors did, and as Wifey and I often did. Right outside the rec room windows was the Big Creek Valley and a great view of Red Rock and folds and folds of blue hazy mountains: a constantly changing, always startling visual feast. Yeah, it was The View that we bought. The house was a fright.

For a while, we enjoyed the tainted glamour of the house's reputation.

"Oh, you folks tuck the bootlegger's house," new acquaintances would say. "Best bootlegger in the county. They never got him, you know."

When we took out the metal flue for the pipe of the wood-burning stove that we had eliminated, we discovered that there was no real attic—just a crawl space big enough for maybe a snake. When we went through the floor with the new staircase, we found out all we would ever want to know about the main floors. Then I tore out a wall and connected two back-to-back closets and found out about the interior walls. One new window taught me about the outside walls, the insulation, even certain wiring details. Studs on sixteen inch centers. Impressive to me.

At one end of the house, there was a greenhouse, and below that an area we dubbed "The Bunker." Both were peculiar voids—about five feet wide, and across the whole end of the house—with a square opening in the concrete floor of the greenhouse leading down into The Bunker. The Bunker was concrete all around, except for a door in one end where part of the cement wall had been torn out. The greenhouse would heat up to oven temperatures in summer. And the cool of The Bunker met that heat in that square opening. I later learned that The Bunker had been a cistern years ago, and that the greenhouse had been added recently to make the place more "salable." Everything in the house had been something else, it seemed, or was about to be transformed by me. That end of the house especially bothered me.

Then one day a neighbor dropped by, and the bootlegger story came up, and she said something that changed everything.

"He was the best bootlegger in the county," she recited. "They never got him. That was because of the secret room."

"Secret room?" Wifey asked, just getting in ahead of me.

"Oh yes. Oh my yes!" She was a sweet little old lady, diminutive and low key, but she had our attention. "He had a secret room. No matter how many times they raided, they never found any hooch! He had a secret room, all right."

"Where was it?" I had to ask.

"Nobody ever knew. It was a secret! Folks that lived here after the bootlegger left never found it. The folks you bought it from never found it. Sheriff never found it. But it was here. And I bet it's still here," she said, as her eyes, large and suspicious, scanned the limits of what she could see from the couch. I could tell she wanted to search the place.

Well! A secret room! My mind grabbed that phrase and took it right inside and dragged it under the covers and cuddled with it and hugged it and stroked it and petted it and...Never mind. I seized that phrase and gave it complete access to what was left of my sanity.

A secret room. Mentally, I rummaged through every floor and wall and ceiling, every nook and cranny, crevice and crack—everything that used to be or still was or could have been a place, a room. I accounted for every cubic inch of that house as it was in its present incarnation; then I speculated on what might have been or must have been. I combed though it, sifted it, riffled it. And I could not find the secret room in any form or tense.

I reasoned that I would have to seek that magical void at midnight during a thunderstorm, perhaps by torchlight. I could hear the heavy music. I could imagine cold, clammy air, echoing voices, creaking doors, ghostly, clinking beer bottles in the deep shadows. I considered asking Wifey to put on a diaphanous negligee, light a candle, and go down into the cellar, searching, in the wee small hours of the morning. Barefooted, of course. I thought of inviting a crew of weird psychics with strange instruments to come spend the night and find the room. I imagined finding dusty blueprints in the basement archives of the old county courthouse. There would have to be an innocent looking, spooky little kid saying, "I see dead soldiers. They're here."

"It's probably gone now, " said Wifey. "It's probably a closet or bedroom, or maybe it's the laundry room or The Bunker."

"None of them is secret. This was a secret room."

"If you insist."

And I did. I insisted. But then I gravitated toward sanity. The room was changed, exposed, no longer secret. That was all. It was not a case of moving a particular stone in the fireplace and causing a wall to spin around, revealing a room, a skeleton, and empty bottles. It was not as if I could swivel the base of a candlestick and make a panel slide off to the left and betray some skulking, hidden hole in the wall leading into a dark tunnel, down to a cave, perhaps, or into some forbidden sanctuary. It was unlikely that a trap door under the washer or dryer led to mysterious steps—down into a passage deep inside the mountain where a cache of forgotten booze awaited discovery. There was no trunk anywhere filled with ill-gotten gains, and nobody was out there in a cell somewhere waiting for the day he could return and penetrate that passage and retrieve his booty! Nobody was buried in the yard, probably, beneath a flower bed, moldering away.

Maybe there had been another opening in the cement of the floor of The Bunker—or on the West side of the house, a void under the huge stone that I could never move.

It occurred to me that the more certain I was that there was no longer any secret room in our house, the more uncomfortable I became with the general aura of the place. I began to feel the room. I made jokes about it; I dreamed about it; I heard it in the night, pulsating. I would look toward the place as I turned from the mailbox out on the highway, and there was a vapor or a tiny cloud, an entity, a soul—something that said, "Hidden Void." Once, I was playing with a compass in the back yard, and the needle went crazy and spun and tilted, then settled on a direction that could not possibly have been North. But soon I was taught that North was indeed where that compass pointed, and rest was hysteria on my part. The bootlegger, whose ghost I was convinced was on site, was alive and well and had opened a liquor store in Missouri. That came out in the local newspaper.

"So go to Missouri," said Wifey, "and find him, and ask him where the room was. But you've got to quit creeping around the house in the middle of the night."

"Suppose I did that," I challenged her. "And suppose there was no secret room."

"If there *was* no secret room, then there *is* no secret room, and you can move on to some other obsession." Wifey had her feet on the ground, and I knew there was nothing but ground under her feet—because I had checked all of it by then.

"Thing is, Dear, there is a secret room now, whether there was one then or not! And, since I am the one who believes in it, I am the one who will never find it, making it non-secret, and spoiling the whole thing."

"There's a name for that," said Wifey. "I'm going to look it up as soon as I have time."

The neighbor lady and I became close, because she believed in the room, too. I told her that I could feel the room's presence, that there were cold spots in the house, that unexplained noises filled the night, that there was a mysterious throbbing—always in the other end of the house, no matter where I was. And she did not laugh at me. She nodded, bug-eyed, and she shivered just a little. Together, we stared into space. This grew. I soon realized that the secret room was as real as it had to be.

"It's all in your head," Wifey concluded. "This secret room is all in your head."

"Precisely."

I use the secret room whenever we have company these days, especially new company. Wifey lets me get away with it, but I know she's not happy about it. Just recently, an old college buddy of mine found me on the Internet, called me on the phone, then rolled into my driveway as I was trying yet another trick to change the shape of the shack. I greeted him and his wife, we hugged , we pounded on each other a little, introductions were made all around, I apologized for the architectural horror, then I led them out back and watched their eyes as The View overwhelmed them. Somewhere, he had a great house and not much of a view; I had this disappointing house and a great view. I let them stand there in awe for a while; Wifey offered refreshments and friendly chit-chat with my buddy's wife; and gradually the sun went down and The View disappeared.

"This was The Bootlegger's House," I told them, "and it had a secret room. And you know, I think it still has."

There was a full moon that night. I don't think they slept a wink.

Auction Action

"Folks'll do just about anything for a little entertainment," the neighbor lady had assured us. "Someone cares to resin up a bow or tune up the old guitar, folks gather, and it's an event. Best thing going, though, is the charity auction. Puts everything together." And the neighbor lady was our source of conventional wisdom, so we listened. After a few months in the mountains, we were game for whatever entertainment we could find.

"The auction," our neighbor said, "is what has become of the feud. You don't have Hatfields and McCoys these days. That all happens at the auction." We liked that scrappy lady, and we trusted her.

Wifey and I looked into the matter, of course, and soon we were regulars at any auction that came up. Wifey has a sweet tooth, and at these auctions (benefiting some local cause) pies and cakes and brownies, candy and cookies, and other baked goodies, always highlighted the sale. Tickets to Branson shows were popular, too, we discovered. Sometimes a musical group would cork up before the action, and there might even be junk food around for me—a hot dog or two. Some Diet Coke. It was altogether pleasing.

Of course, there was the junk: the same junk that was there last time. People would bring something they could spare and donate it to the auction; other folks would bid on the items and buy them and take them home; then when the next charity auction came along, they had something to donate. The money went to The Cause, whatever it was. So the same core backlash of useless junk made the rounds. I think we owned that one wash stand (with linoleum glued to it) about five times. Sometimes a new item—something picked up at a salvage sale in Russellville or Harrison—got into the pile. But it was not important. The Game: that was the important thing.

We were new to the area, but people did not hold it against us long. They had been new in the area themselves not long ago. Very few of the actual "hillbillies" were left when we showed up in the mountains south of Jasper. Around us were former pilots, engineers, doctors, teachers, and nurses, attracted to the hills by the natural beauty and the favorable economics. But at the auctions, the native folks showed up.

"Just don't get into a bidding war with anybody," the neighbor lady had warned. "These people will hold a grudge. You don't want to come out here and beat them at their own game. They know where you live." (She spoke as an outsider, only about a dozen years on the mountain.)

Well! Statements like that put things in a different light! An auction could get interesting in a hurry. So we had to show up. It was a gig (and there were so few gigs). Sooner or later, something could actually happen. We went eagerly to that first memorable auction.

❧

"EEEyuhh Hawwh! Hooo Yuhaaa!" someone screamed into public address system, and the auction to benefit the animal shelter was in progress. Old "Mule" Ferguson was the auctioneer, probably donating his time and his colorful technique. He started each sale with a pretty good impersonation of a mule, and, from what I could see, he sustained throughout the session. Wifey and I settled in with the crowd as it gathered around the auctioneer and leaned in close. This sale seemed special.

At an auction, the bidder has to have a number, registered with the cashier. When he wins a bid and makes a buy, his number and the price of the item are recorded. He settles up later with the cashier, paying for everything he purchased on the day. Wifey registered the number; I acted as a "consultant" and stayed out of the way (and out of the fray). This became our *modus operandi* at all future auctions. (Some of the local folks thought it was unmanly of me, but I was no longer in the mood to worry about such trivia.)

"Mule, we got a pecan pie here about a yard across," the assistant auctioneer/spotter announced. "Let's start it at five!" (This guy is sometimes called a "ring man.")

"EEEEyuhh Hawwwh!" screamed Mule, and then he unleashed a broadside of yodeling babble that made it sound like one of those Russian eggs was for sale. He jabbered up one side of the crowd and down the other, picking up subtle movements here and there, screaming, and quickly accelerating the pace of things. Very shortly, the price was $12, and the pie was sold. Two ladies had locked horns over the pecan pie, just briefly, and one of them now claimed her treasure. Wifey didn't blink, mainly because she had seen two other pecan pies and a few cherry and apple ones, and she was looking for a deal. I could tell that the auction had just begun, and it was going to take a while. This was just a warm-up.

I want to go on record about one thing: I did not, at any time during the proceedings, understand one word that Old Mule uttered. Well, not until the end. It was like Bob Dylan on speed; it was like Mel Tillis with Novocain in his tongue; it was like Rap run backwards at an accelerated speed. I was a mile behind everybody else, and I did not know what was for sale or what was being said. I kept wanting to say, "Excuse me. Would you repeat that?" But from the rhythm of the thing, I could tell basically what was going on. Sorta. And after a few go-rounds, I was able to determine that two ladies were having a feud, just like the neighbor lady said. They were eccentric-looking, middle-aged women, and it was obvious to me that they were dangerous. In fact, the neighbor lady herself appeared at my elbow and said, "Watch those two. You'll see what I mean." Before my eyes, the two women mutated into toothless hillbillies with old muzzle loaders, taking potshots at each other, down in the holler by the crick! If Mule broke off jabbering and let out a scream, I knew that one of them had won a battle.

Part of an old wood-burning stove went to a guy in the biggest pair of bib overalls I had ever seen, but then an oak high chair came up, and the two ladies clashed. They glared at each other, and I could see blood in their eyes. They wielded their number cards in slashing strokes, and before long that little chair was pulling in fifteen dollars for the animal shelter. The women tried to hide it, but I could see that the victor was acting smug and the loser was ticked off.

Wifey nailed an apple pie right away, and Mule nearly popped a vein with his primal scream. Five dollars. The two competing ladies just stared at each other and let Wifey have the pie. All later pies went for $7 or more. A box of old nuts and bolts, rusty screen door springs, and half a can of WD40 went for $2 to a guy wearing a John Deere cap. Nothing from the ladies on that. A busted bicycle, a busted exercise bicycle, a busted propane stove, and several second-generation farm tools—also busted—went for perfectly good money. The two ladies did some of the lower bidding, but others took the items.

Local merchants had contributed sacks of dog food and other products of value. A local woodworker had contributed a hutch that had Wifey's attention, big time! I was able to fix her with my glittering eye as the bids reached the $60 mark, she backed off, and the hutch went for $190! Out of our league. The hat lady took it.

"Mule, we got brownies!" said the spotter, holding up a huge plate of scrumptious looking brown squares. "They've got frosting, too!"

"Eeeaaauuuhh Graw!" shrieked Mule.

"Five dollars," said Wifey. I thought she seemed calm about the whole thing.

"Yammer bladdle graphen nugglede chow clamyel nuggle nuggle nuggle..." replied Mule, I believe, and the next thing

I knew my wife was bidding fifteen dollars for the brownies. Mule threw his hat up in the air and jabbered it down, leaping and pointing.

One of the serious ladies said, "Twenty dollars!" And she eyeballed Wifey. Wifey withdrew quietly, and the bidding ended at $20. Both of the competing ladies looked at Wifey and accused her of murder, child abuse, and insider trading—it was all there in their eyes. I can read faces. Our family was always full of good face readers. I was relieved.

❧

Well, it went on and on. Wifey ended up with the apple pie, some cookies, two sacks of dog food for the shelter, a batch of brownies (different ones), a nice cherry pie, one pecan pie, and some kind of a plate that meant nothing to me. (It was empty.) Seat covers, an old sewing machine, a set of old hotel dishes (chipped), a rusty shovel, a snag of computer components, seven hundred cedar jewel boxes in one lot (just in case you wanted to take a booth at an upcoming crafts show), the left front door of a sedan from back in the sixties somewhere, eighty-seven eight-track tapes, a few cans of unlabeled paint—all went to someone whose particular plight made it seem reasonable. (Not Wifey. Say Amen!)

But I was watching those two feuding ladies. One of them got the George Foreman grill after a fierce set-to; the other one just had to have the peach cobbler, and paid for it, too! They nearly broke into a fistfight over the Bobby Vinton tickets, I swear. I almost sidled over and warned them about the steepness of the parking lot at Bobby's place there in Branson, but I kept quiet. I could hear teeth gritting, and there were low growls. I thought one of them hissed, at least twice, but I was never sure. I could only imagine what was going to happen if they had tickets for Andy Williams. I stepped clear. Lawrence Welk tickets would have caused it to go nuclear! And Lawrence is dead.

In fact, I could see that a lot of the men were pulling back now, away from those women. Even Wifey, who stayed into each bid only to the limits of prudence and logic, seemed to stay low, in both bid and posture. It was war, all right. Those two women were after blood. I mumbled a silent prayer about Wifey—a fierce competitor unaccustomed to losing.

One of the women had a fruit-clustered straw hat with a red sash around it and dropping over the side: peculiar thing to look at. The other one was dressed in a bright yellow jogging outfit, and with the size of her, she looked like a school bus sitting there. I later learned that people really interested in bidding dressed to be seen easily. When I mentioned that to my wife, she told me not to hold my breath. I am still working on that remark.

"Eeeeuh Haahh!" screamed the auctioneer, and then a volley of grunting bellows, as if the "mule" in question had fallen into a well full of hornets' nests. "E Yudy yyuh dunbyk bunghy hungny!" And then, of course, "Yabba dabba doo" or some such prattle.

An absolutely terrible lamp had emerged from the pile. Someone, it seemed, had retrieved the melted trash from the bottom of the burning barrel out back (common local practice), and wired it and painted it and found a way to put a lampshade on it. Roaches would not live in this thing; spiders would spin their webs elsewhere; rats would throw this lamp out of the attic; self-respecting dust would not accumulate on this lamp. It was bad.

And the two feuding women elbowed everybody else out of the area and took over. This was the climactic moment in the auction, I could tell. It was as if they had stepped into the street at high noon, their numbered cards at the ready, their steely eyes cold and sullen. Old Mule sensed it, too, and he became so animated that I feared for him. He ripped off his string tie and popped open his shirt; he rolled up his sleeves as he screamed; he made little jumps in the direction of first one lady, then the other, as they locked horns. Ten dollars, then fifteen. Do I hear twenty? Twenty. Now five. Twenty-five. Thirty dollar bill? Now thirty-five. I could not really understand, but I could sense the thing—feel the prices rise. People gathered close, and the competing women locked eyes on each other. There were moans and gasps as the bids went higher—even applause, sighs, and little cheers.

And then, just when I was becoming highly amused, "Forty dollars!" yelled my beloved wife.

"Eeeyukgn gloph ooooeeeyaak!" I screamed.

Everything went dead quiet, and people stared at me. I sat down fast. I got one of those "Who the hell are you?" stares from the entire crowd. Wifey about kicked my legs out from under me. Then Old Mule let out one of HIS screams, followed by yammer-de-jabber-de-chatter at a pitch and intensity unmatched by anything else of the day. And I was grateful. His scream, music to me this time, shifted the attention back to the three competing female auction warriors. The yellow bus lady and the hat lady exchanged a glance, and I could see instant concurrence—conspiracy, collusion!

"Fifty dollars!" the school bus woman yelled, and both women turned and eyeballed Wifey. I turned and eyeballed Wifey, too, I must relate, and we had a moment there. Wifey said nothing. She just smiled and waved her little card.

"We've got fifty-five dollars!" shouted the ring man.

"Eeeeyuh glungh waawwwk!" screamed Mule Ferguson, leaping in the air. I didn't hear anything after that. It all went into slow motion. I went numb. The hideous lamp was raised up and waved around. Men in the crowd backed up even more, and the two competing women, allies now, pooled their money and came after Wifey. I was terrified. I grasped my wallet and backed up against a tree. Arms waved, bidder numbers flashed, everything became a blur. I became short of breath.

More incomprehensible gibberish, then suddenly a triumphant scream from Old Mule. At last he said English words that I could understand. "All in? All done? Sold to the lady for $95!"

I could not look. I shut my eyes. I could see a thick packet of my money on little wings, flying off into the sunset. My next phone call would be to Ripley's, because I just knew that the ugliest lamp in the world was coming home with me. And I could imagine a fight actually initiated by me in our car on the way home. I was near collapse.

❧

"I like your style, kid," I heard a raspy female voice say from too close for comfort. It was the woman with the hat. I knew she was not talking to me.

"Thank you," said Wifey.

"But we had to take that lamp from you." The school bus-looking lady was there, too, and they had the lamp. A crippling wave of relief hit me and weakened my knees. It was a miracle.

"It's $95 for the animals," said the hat lady, "and it was the last item of interest."

"Pretty much my thinking," said Wifey. "Hate the lamp. Love the animals."

"We'll ditch it at the Baptist Youth auction next week. I'm Madge Colstad, and this is Ma...uh...Thelma Wainwright. Who are you?"

And the three of them proceeded to have a round of giggling and girl talk that about made me sick. They hugged on each other, exchanged phone numbers, gave each other high fives, and I don't know what all. The yellow one, it turned out, was the founder of the animal shelter; the other one was her best friend. And now the three of them run around all over the mountains with each other, looking for more mischief.

I looked all over that crowd for our neighbor that auction day, but she was gone. The first tiny cracks were developing in the structure of my trust in her. (I liked her anyway.) I started to understand that I was going to have to have an open mind to live in the hills, and definitely take a "wait and see" posture.

The Craft It Takes

In the hinterlands, perfectly innocent objects, such as sticks and stones, rounds of timber, empty beer cans, and rusty barbed wire, run the risk of being espied by an itinerant crafter. Soon, in creative processes that baffle those of us who are not "crafty," these inanimate things become animated. They are turned into little characters, working windmills, ladies' hats, model canoes, mobiles, automobiles, insects, birds, tools, and knick-knacks. A few snowbound winter nights, a glue gun, a soldering iron, a wood-burning tool, some paint, and imagination: then, a miracle. Crafts Show, here we come!

Wifey and I had always been fascinated with crafts shows, even in the city. On any Saturday, we could, if we chose, wander through rows of booths set up in cordoned-off parts of the city—whole streets or vacant lots, sometimes whole neighborhoods, devoted to the crafts. A broom maker would be there somewhere; a cobbler would be cobbling; a cooper would be cooping; usually quilters were quilting and smiths were smithing, and all of "Santa's Helpers" were making elves of themselves. We were relieved when we discovered that the Ozark countryside was full of such wonders also. Someone somewhere had probably taken a tuna can, a bobby pin, and a piece of bamboo and made a musical instrument, and we had to see it. If someone had embroidered a Mona Lisa, we wanted to be there.

We met Pete Blanchart at a crafts show. He had booked space at War Eagle, a real federal case event in northwest Arkansas, and he had wooden lawn furniture that he had taken from tree to finished product all on his own.

"This was a cedar tree when I first saw it," he said of one of his finest pieces. "Some of these other folks are phonies—go to a lumber yard. Me? I find the perfect tree, cut it down, saw it up, age the wood, and then work my magic." He was "right proud."

"I like this table," said Wifey. "Did you design it?"

"Design and build all my own stuff. Ever bit of it."

Well, it was photographable, and I had my camera along, and I worked for an angle. But that was a bad idea, and I should have known better.

"That's a nice camera," Pete said, "but I wouldn't use it around here if I was you. There's a lot of pirate activity, and these crafters will jump all over you if they think you're stealin' an idea."

We had run into that before. Neither of us had a crafter bone in our body. Threads and yarns were safe from Wifey, and most hammer & nail things were safe from me. Beer cans remained beer cans; cedar stumps remained cedar stumps. We could not help even the humblest, most helpless looking piece of debris become anything else. We were at the show to get out of the house, and when we saw something cute, Wifey wanted a picture of it so that we could say, "Look at this cute thing we saw at the crafts show." And tell our friends.

"They got on an old boy here last year, and I thought they were gonna have him arrested. He had a video camera, and that old gal that makes scarecrows outa bamboo, burlap, and bananas about gelded him! Some of us smoothed it over and explained. But we don't want no picture-takin' around here."

"Fair enough," I said, putting my camera away. "Do you get a lot of lawn furniture counterfeiters here?"

"Hey, you think that's funny, but, you know those two old boys in the A-frame on Scenic Seven?"

"We do. They're friends of ours," said Wifey.

"Well, of course I don't want to bad-mouth nobody, but those fellas flat out stole my chair design. And they're sellin' 'em from their store to every tourist that comes along! By-God pirates." (Many tourists frequent our area—for the scenery and the canoe adventures on the Buffalo River.)

"Really! I know they're in the business: cedar furniture, indoor and outdoor. They're doing well, from what I know. Which chair of yours did they copy?" I had to know.

"You're sittin' on it right now."

Both Wifey and I had checked with Pete, of course, before we sat down on the lawn furniture. We had introduced ourselves, and he knew that we were practically neighbors. We were just a ridge or two away through the mountains—two miles as the crow flies, eight miles on the roads. But it was polite to get permission to try out the furniture, neighbor or not. But , alas, what I was sitting in was an Adirondack chair, pure and simple.

"Okay, you built this chair," I said, "but you say you designed it?"

"Every angle and curve. Figured all the stresses and counter-stresses, all the dynamics of the thing. Worked on it all one winter. Got it just right. People seem to like 'em."

Wifey is from New York. Long Island. And I'm a Minnesota boy. And both of us did a lot of time in Texas, and I was a proud citizen of Iowa and then Nebraska for a while there. Together we have been to all of the lower forty-eight states and Hawaii. In England, Scotland and Wales, we have seen Adirondack chairs; in the Adirondacks and the Rockies and the Smokies and the Ozarks—in the woods and by the lakes and rivers. Adirondack chairs everywhere: the same laid-back design everywhere. Wifey had even, on a whim, built an Adirondack chair herself, following a pattern she was mailed, probably by one of Martha Stewart's co-conspirators. We knew about Adirondack chairs. TV woodworkers do shows about them. We had one on our deck at the time.

"Pete, I wouldn't get too upset with the guys at the A-frame," I said.

Right away I got a kick from Wifey. I could tell that I was supposed to shut up immediately and not bring the subject up again. And I was willing. Really. This was embarrassing, and I wanted to wander off into the crowd and forget the whole thing. I deserved kicking. Wifey was right. (Do you know how that hurts?)

"I'm not upset. I just want to get the two of them in my sights. You can't go around stealin' another man's art, his ideas, his life's blood. I make a living sellin' this cedar furniture."

"Why not have the boys at the A-frame market your stuff for you?"

"How do you think they got their first chair? They bought one of mine, and they've been knockin' 'em off ever since. I may sue!"

"But, you know, " I said, "this chair is called..."

I got kicked. It hurt, too. And Wifey was right. I should let it go.

"This chair is a work of art," I said, "and I'd hate to think someone would steal your idea. Ever spend any time back East—New England—up in there?"

"Spent my whole life right here in the mountains. I never went there, and I didn't leave nothin' there, and I ain't goin' back there to get nothin' I didn't leave there in the first place."

Well, he had that wrong, too, but I kept quiet. A triple-backlash double negative hits a nerve with an old English teacher, but I stayed all impulses and tried to change the subject.

"Boy, those bean-bag chairs over there are wild!" I said, gesturing toward the West, into the sun.

"Knock-offs, every one of 'em," sneered Pete. "They're just makin' what somebody else came up with years and years ago. They got no respect, no originality. They're the sorriest strain of crafters."

"Yeah, you see bean-bag chairs everywhere."

Wifey got out of her Adirondack chair, and I got out of mine, and we started making sounds like people about to drift away into the crowd. I had a small limp going, because of being kicked so hard, and probably because of being laid out in that hard chair.

"Why'd you wanna know if I'd ever been back East. Somethin' in my accent?"

"Naw. You haven't got an accent. I was just wondering." I noticed an inexorable force pulling at my arm, moving me in the general direction of "to hell out of there"! "Well, we've got to get out of your hair now and move on. Still haven't seen that whole row of stuff over there. But we'll see you soon and often. Nice to meet one of our neighbors."

"You see your buddies at that A-frame, tell 'em to watch out. What they've done is very unpopular in these parts. A man may not have much beyond his creative spark, but I say that when you put in the time and effort, and design something that folks like, it ought to be your own."

"I wouldn't give it another thought, if I were you. First thing you know you'll be able to see that chair all over the country. And you'll know you contributed something to the world."

"Know what I'm gonna do?" he yelled after us, "I'm gonna get a patent. Maybe I'll get rich."

"You could give it a name," I offered, being towed away backwards. " Lazy Boy or something cute like that."

Wifey barked my shin at that point and physically dragged me away toward some varnished sumac and corn cob bathroom accessories set up in a tepee a few yards away.

Secretly Young

When I first cast my weakening gaze upon The County Senior Citizens Center, I knew that there would be a day when I would be dragged there by my reluctant hand for surrender ceremonies. I checked for the stench of old age (which I just knew would be there, but was not) and for the familiar smells of institution food (food which I had eaten all my teaching life and in school before). Then I went outside and waited for Wifey in the porch swing. I fled, really.

"I am just a tourist here," I said out loud.

Months later, I was maneuvered back there and efficiently signed in as a guest. Wifey seemed to know how it was done. I hesitated—resisted—because I was simply not old enough for this place. They had geezers, and they had them bad. I had retired early, and I did not feel that I had the numbers to be at this place legitimately. Not quite, anyway. I did not wish to be around a bunch of old people. I did not belong there. But we had lunch, and people were polite to me, and they addressed Wifey by her first name. She seemed to know a few of them.

I could be like a mascot, I thought, if they nailed me. They could call me "Kid" or something, and I could help people out of their chairs, or help them mince about with six inch steps. It would be okay to visit occasionally—not to get involved, or anything—just get my feet wet a little. And, God help me, I liked the food.

Wifey tricked me into visiting the rec room, and there she challenged a man to a game of pool—with me! "I am legally blind," he said as we met. Then he beat me down like a dog.

On my way out, they had a picture puzzle laid out and working, and I couldn't walk past that. I fell into that project until Wifey towed me away. My "date" was a little old lady, and we worked well together. Puzzle people know about such things.

This grew. I started really enjoying the food and the company—developed friendships, led at first by Wifey, but then I found friends of my own as the weeks passed. I shot a little pool. I kept signing in as a guest, but this was getting serious. I was not old. In fact, I was feeling younger each day. It was like the relationship with the neighbor lady up on the hill: I could bask in the glow without *becoming*, could I not? No need to embrace "geezerdom" and join it like it was the Elks club or something! Or go play Bingo! You see, I was only "technically" qualified: I had the birthdays, but I was secretly young.

❧

And then the management grabbed me. I knew I was going to be tossed out on my ear sooner or later. You can't go around faking your age for long. People are not stupid.

"Wanna fill out some paper work for me?" she said.

"Sure," I said matter-of-factly. But I knew that this was it. I could see it in the *Harrison Daily Times*. "Fake Geezer Nabbed at Area Senior Center!" But Harrison was a big town. Our little local paper would print something like, "Millers Named Shepherd Family of Year." They did not like controversy and would not mention such an unpleasantness.

"Before you fill out the papers, though," said the manager lady, "there is an interview. Can you sit down for a minute?"

"If I go to the restroom before we begin, yes." So, I was excused! Me! A teacher! I almost asked for a hall pass.

In the restroom I glanced at the mirror. Uh-oh. Not exactly young. But not old. Certainly not *that* old. This hair was darker than the stuff the barber recently claimed he cut off my head. That had to be "throw down" hair. Why was I doing this?

"I am ready for the pop quiz," I told the manager when I returned and took a seat.

"Let's call it a conversation."

"Good." I was busted, though: I knew it in my youthful heart. She was gonna toss me.

"First of all," she said, "CAN YOU HEAR ME?" Really loud.

"Yes."

"Good. Can you see me?" She waved.

"Yes. Guess I'm outa here, huh?"

"Not yet. Many of our people can both see and hear. How long have you been a member of the AARP?" She seemed to have information.

"Long time. They nabbed me when I was fifty. Are they communists or something?"

"No. I don't think we have communists anymore. Anyway, that part checks out." She looked at a paper of some sort. "How well are you sleeping lately?" She didn't look at me.

"Not very well."

"Aha." She made a mark or two on her clipboard. "How much do you eat late in the day, for your evening meal?"

"Well, supper isn't much. Very little meat. Indigestion and gas. I'm lucky to get anything down at all, with all those telemarketers calling. I like to cuss 'em out!"

"That is normal," she said, marking a check list. "And do you get up at about 4:30 a.m.?"

"Why, yes. And maybe another time or two."

"Do you contribute to any charities?"

"Not any more."

"And how many pounds of address labels do you have at home?"

Well, I knew what she meant. Every charity on Earth prints up address labels and sends them to old people, begging for money. "About ten pounds. I had to burn a few boxes of them six weeks back. I get about five envelopes a day. I sent ten dollars to one outfit two years ago."

"That's a clincher, you know. You're old now. You are being *targeted*! You, Sir, have arrived." She smiled and shook my hand.

"Thank you," I said dryly.

"It's a rite of passage. You might consider keeping those

address labels," she said. "We have an annual contest to see who has the most. You could compete. Who turned you in?"

"I think it was a paralyzed veteran merchant marine outfit. Ten lousy dollars, and the next week I heard from seventeen "sibling" charities. They turned me over to The Syndicate."

"Well, hang on to those things—just for the fun of it. You could paper your bedroom."

"Who's got the record? In the contest, I mean."

"Emma Brown. Thirty-five pounds at weigh-in—but she had purged six months before. A lady in Russellville has the state record."

"Well, I guess I could give it a shot."

"Excellent! Now, how do you like our food?"

"Not bad."

"Really?" She eyed me suspiciously.

"Yeah. I can eat here."

"Yep. You're old, all right. Want to get into some art lessons, ceramics classes, quilt hooking?"

"Not yet."

"Want to sign up for the shuttle bus to WalMart?"

"I'm gonna save that for later."

"We check blood pressures once a month. Need to know if you've got a pulse."

When I laughed, she was pleased that I got the joke. Made a check mark.

"I'll try to have a pulse at least once a month," I said cleverly.

She rose, and I did, too—and that alone would have been enough. "You are a gentleman! I believe you fit the profile, Sir. You are a Senior Citizen."

"Heck," I said, "I got my first Senior Citizens' Discount when I was 55—in a buffet in Carson City, Nevada. Depressing, but I got over it."

"Well, I will handle all the rest now. Just give me those papers."

"I haven't filled them out."

"Oh, your wife took care of that last week. I was just pulling your chain here."

I knew that. I have an instinct for these things. Wifey had been what us old teachers call "Absent: Unexcused" lately. I knew she was up to something. Besides, there were only two of us at our place on the mountain, and when one of us was gone, the other noticed. I knew.

"Really: you're already signed up. You're one of us now. Relax. Go limp."

"Right."

That was when I surrendered. How bad could it be, right? Nice people, good food, puzzles, pool table. I had evidently already made my "final arrangements." I decided to roll over for it. I could keep my soul, too.

"Well, do I get a certificate or diploma or anything?" I asked, pulling away to go think

"No, but there's a shawl with your name on it. Welcome aboard."

Later, I sat alone in the porch swing, just dangling my feet, thinking and waiting. It was as if I were up top, at Scenic Point, maybe, or in my own backyard, peering over the edge into the wonder of it all, like a tourist, smiling.

Moving Double-Dog's Piano

When I felt the wet tongue of Double-Dog Darrell's she-wolf in my left ear, I knew I had visitors. I screamed, dropped my rugged man's garden trowel, and leaped straight in the air about three feet. (I was younger then.) I landed cursing.

"Damn, Darrell, I wish you wouldn't do that."

There were four wolves in the yard, and Double-Dog was there on his knobby horse, fully costumed for the moment, a crow perched on his shoulder. He was tall and dark and saturnine. He was all about impact, and he had made his entrance.

"Yer too easy to walk up on. Better pay attention. Never know." There was New Hampshire in his vowels (from long ago), and Texas, and Ozark.

He liked to be noticed suddenly, like a snake. Today he was regaled in outlaw livery: Willie Nelson/Woody Allen, but more Latino. He had a serape woven into the get-up. The horse stood still, and the wolves faced away from the horse in four directions, watching, like Secret Service agents. Double-Dog wanted people to think something sinister was going on.

"Damn! Where did you even *come* from?"

"Down the hollow, by the stream, at the mouth of the cave, among the boulders..." He grinned.

"I know where you live. But, damn! Do you have to sneak up on a man like that?"

"Snuck up here on a horse—with all my dogs runnin' wild, in broad daylight, with a goat trailin' behind. You gotta pay more attention to things." He had scolded me about such things before.

I looked around for whatever else might have crept up on me while I was engrossed in Wifey's day lily bed, and there was Monica Goat, by the white fence, munching a weed for me, her long ears flapping in the wind. Monica was a Nubian goat, but she thought she was a wolf.

Oh, they were wolves, all right, mostly: very much a pack, complete with a social order, everyone cast in a role. (From intimate experience, I knew they were 97% wolf, bred locally in an operation later available to Internet shoppers!) Double-Dog was one of them, really. His "handle" was something he had picked up after moving to the mountains. At first he had run around with two dogs; now it was four wolves. Double.

"What brings you up here out of your lair?"

"How's your back?"

Aha. Something in Double-Dog's bailiwick was heavy, and I was elected. I knew that in a moment or two I would be obligated.

"Back's fine," I said. I saw him glance at the house. "Step down. Just don't let my wife see you. She's still mad." But the curtains moved, and then the Venetian blinds closed. Wifey knew.

He smiled and stroked his chin pensively: a pose. "Hmmm. Four months tomorrow. Pretty good." He dismounted glancing again at the house.

Double-Dog had legions of what he called "former friends," my wife among them. The man seemed to have no staying power when it came to friendships. Sooner or later (usually sooner), he would say or do something that alienated people. With Wifey it had been an exchange about his Thorazine and her Estrogen, each recommending large dosages to the other. Shame, too. He had noticed that Wifey was attractive, and he had been impressed (like most men), but they were getting along. Then, irretrievable words, oaths, and vows—an epic rhubarb—and the whole thing was spoiled. Another story completely. Their feud would last another month or so. Double-Dog was proud of its longevity.

There were other legends and lies in circulation. With the next door neighbor, a school board member, there were remarks, then war, supposedly.. Double-Dog's offer to re-configure the school system and punch up the curriculum with "heretofore unknown leadership"—all at a public meeting—failed to amuse The Establishment, especially its leaders. All over the hills, supposedly, there were restraining orders, "No Trespassing" signs, locked gates and doors and fences—all with his name on them. Sometimes his name was there literally: "This means you, Double-Dog!" There were places where he drew gunfire, and there were places where he would need every one of his wolves. He moved like a dark stain through the community. At least that's the way Darrell told it.

I did not have anything against him at that time; it was just uncomfortable being around him out in the open. Indeed, you never know. Mine fields are safer. There was an atmosphere—a plug of bad air—around Double-Dog: screen doors closed, children were summoned indoors, shades were drawn, women folded their arms and clutched collars to their throats. Like that. It was uncomfortable being a part of that, even for a short while. Uncomfortable, but somehow worth it.

A stranger might think this an exaggeration. After all, this is the Twenty-First Century. We are civilized now. Ask anyone. But it would be hard to exaggerate Double-Dog's distinct, very calculated effect on people. (I always thought he was going for the "Wheelbarrow Steve" image—a hermit who once lurked around Round Top mountain and allegedly went after a woman caveman style!)

He wanted people to flinch or recoil—to drop their silverware and do a spit take, or go bug-eyed at the sight of him. And he wanted that to continue, with each gesture, each word, each outrage. The rumors about the supernatural thing were probably untrue. But gossipers said that he had squatted on people's land, lived in caves, put moves on other men's wives, led children in rebellions, introduced radical religious ideas, caused and encouraged doubt in people who really needed beliefs. One group of sweet little old ladies had evidence that he was a warlock; voodoo and human sacrifice were mentioned over Canasta tables at the nursing home; local women in the grocery stores kept their carts between themselves and Double-Dog as a matter of course. He had been seen on that horse in the dead of night—riding in the moonlight like the Headless Horseman! He was suspected of things. And he was so pleased. By the time I met him, Double-Dog Darrell had already ascended from Man to Myth.

I, of course, knew him and his games, and he was just fine when he had his medication or, as the neighbor lady suggested, some pot to smoke. The Veteran's Administration tried to keep the pills coming on schedule, but up in the hills tight schedules suffer. Sometimes, in a gap between supply and demand, and Double-Dog would have a relapse, unrestrained by the chemicals that made him human. Thus, he had many, many "former friends." The marijuana? Purely rumor, I am almost certain. I never saw any around him.

"So, what's new?" I said to him. (Better yet, *What heavy thing must I lift?*)

He handed me a jar of peanut butter (USDA peanut butter), and we sat down. He kept me in peanut butter because the government supplied it to him, and he correctly discerned that it was legal tender on my part of the mountain. He was spending it now, buying my back. It was good for both of us. (Our excesses, no matter how trivial, trap us.)

"For that you get to help me. I own a piano," he told me, "and it is being held hostage by former friends of mine. I need you to help me get it back." He pulled out a large brown envelope with "Hostage Piano Operation" printed on it in red marker.

Immediately I had visions of fleeing in the darkness along the cliffs with a piano strapped to my back and bullets flying and wolves howling and barbed wire grabbing at me. (I have a flair for melodrama myself.)

"Count me in," I said bravely, posing as a loyal friend and

a courageous, honorable man. I had no trouble believing that someone would actually be holding a piano hostage, if Double-Dog owned the piano. "Who's holding said piano?"

"It's over on Smith Mountain at the Wainwright place. I can't go there. There's a court order. Had a little problem with the Wainwrights four years back."

I started to speak, but Double-Dog stopped me. "Don't ask!"

I wasn't going to ask. I had heard the stories and seen the bullet holes. People shoot some up in the hills. Old Wainwright knew how to shoot, and he probably put those bullets where he wanted them. Still, they had been sincere bullets—locally famous bullets, one of which had gone through Double-Dog and into a tree. There were stories about his home treatment of his wound, his miraculous recovery, mountain folk remedies, all amid ice storms and snow and cold. All I saw was bullet holes in a tree up near the Wainwright place.

"Anyway, I can't go there, but you can. Connivin' Ivan has set up an arrangement. I have to stay four hundred yards away, but you and a few other guys I've got together have been granted permission to go in and get it out. It's how it's done here."

Connivin' Ivan was The Mayor of the Mountains. He was a drop-out, like a lot of us in the hills from Houston, Dallas, L. A., Chicago, Fort Worth, Las Vegas, Milwaukee (pilots and engineers, nurses and teachers, accountants and professors)—retired and re-located. He had been a county sheriff, a mayor, a councilman, and a businessman, and he could swing deals: he could get disparate entities together and get things done—land deals, marital deals, etc. He had been called in to negotiate the release of Double-Dog's piano, and there was a deal in the works: a delicate set-up, but an agreeable, viable transaction.

"But how...?"

"Don't ask."

"Right."

"I get my piano, Wainwright gets rid of me AND the piano, you get peanut butter, the Spender Boys get money, and the other guys owe me favors."

"What's in it for Connivin' Ivan?"

"He gets to connive. There's no downside. The guy's good."

"I believe you."

"Ivan worked inside a Texas prison once: cooled down a riot and got people to back down and still save face. This should be a piece of cake." Famous last words.

There were a lot of Viet Nam veterans in the hills, and all of them seemed to have problems with women. When flashbacks and hot flashes clash, it is complicated. Connivin' Ivan could help. He had recovered Double-Dog's poetry manuscripts when they were held hostage by another of Double-Dog's former friends: an operation which included the local constabulary, the Baptists, and a well digger with a wooden leg. And, of course, a woman. Another story completely. There was PMS involved, and Post Traumatic Stress Disorder, and poetry—a volatile mix. It made Connivin' Ivan locally famous: the consummate arbiter.

❦

I agreed to the gig, mainly because of the peanut butter, but also because of an instinct of mine. When someone is kept human by medicine, you have to be careful about refusing to do things. Details of time and place were already written down on a piece of yellow paper that Double-Dog pulled out of the giant "Operations" envelope, and I made promises. You never know.

One of the wolves, then all of the wolves bristled and focused, and I quickly looked down the road toward the little church about a quarter mile away. A white car was maneuvering in the gravel parking area in front of the church. The sheriff. The car paused, and I supposed that we were receiving some scrutiny. There was a flash: sun-glasses, or maybe binoculars. Double-Dog did not blink. He had noticed the sheriff before even the wolves. Presently, the car moved off in the other direction.

"Look for you Thursday," said Double-Dog. "It will be...legendary!" Then he somehow got back on his horse: he did not spring, he did not bound—he climbed up there, and both he and the horse were unhappy about it. I could tell that both of them were in their golden years, like Wifey and me, and probably the sheriff, for that matter.

❧

On Thursday morning, I put in my appearance at Double-Dog's lair, a mile down in the forested hollow, off the main road, at the base of the cliff. I was greeted by the wolves and the goat, but I knew better than to open my car door until the dominant animal in the pack was present. But then I saw Double-Dog, dressed all in black, posing high atop a house-sized boulder near the cave/spring where he obtained his water. Double-Dog's shanty was one terrace below the main yard: a tiny cabin built of scrap lumber and logs, neat and functional. It had been a stable not long ago, but now it was home to Double-Dog: heated by one open propane burner and four wolves in winter. An ominously rugged ramp was in place, from a platform in the main yard down to the extra-wide Dutch doors of the shanty. I could see the plot. We would back a truck in with the piano and shoot it down to the shanty. The hard part was going to be getting the thing out of Old Wainwright's place.

Nobody else had arrived, and for a moment I thought I was in this adventure alone; but when I slammed my car door, another door slammed right behind me. I turned around, and a familiar stranger was standing there by his Mercedes: familiar because I had seen him before, but a stranger because I did not know him. He had a pair of fine boots, and his jeans were pressed, and he wore yellow leather gloves, brand new. He wore glasses, and they had chains. We nodded and were about to meet when a deep, growling rumble distracted us; as it grew louder and then to deafening proportions, The Spender Boys rolled in with their monster truck: all in camouflage—both men, the truck, even the tires. The Boys were bulky creatures, bearded, dirty, and young: forties, I guessed. Double-Dog did not bother to make introductions. There was a lever-action 30-30 in the back window of the cab, and the mandatory chain saw in the truck bed. Another fellow clad in brownish coveralls drifted into the scene holding a coffee cup. He had been off for a talk with the horse. I knew him and his ten gallon hat.

All we needed now was Connivin' Ivan. And we truly needed him, because this was not a social gathering by any stretch of the imagination. I did not know people like the Spender Boys: I just knew about them. They worked with timber and stone. The guy with the coffee cup was a regular: Cowboy John. He had dropped by and helped me paint my porch the wrong color a year before. And the other fellow? I know very few people who own Mercedes Benz automobiles, but I was curious as to why this one would take his fine car down into that forsaken hollow over a road that looked like an artillery range to help the likes of Double-Dog Darrell—with anything, for any reason. But I remembered that he "owed" Darrell something. I supposed Darrell had killed someone for the Mercedes Nerd, or maybe just disposed of a body, or given him USDA cheese (anything could happen). Maybe they had shared a bottle of hair dye (brown) and bonded. Or, not. And I was immediately aware that nobody knew me very well, and that the others were relative strangers to each other. And Darrell, inside his donut of wolves, was not handing out programs.

Some copious toe sculpture took place at that point. I don't know: it just seemed that we all stood there digging in the dirt with our boots. It wasn't as if someone were about to whip out a twelve-pack and some chips and buffalo wings or anything: it was just not a gathering of "the boys" to help out a buddy. The Spender Boys nudged each other; the guy with the car became preoccupied with a smooth stone near his foot; Cowboy John started using his coffee cup as a repository for great globs of juicy tobacco; Double-Dog just smiled his most enigmatic smile, as if he had caused a "happening" of semi-epic proportions. And there was a silence that made me want to get something going—take charge and move the troops in a direction. But I sensed that such an action might be a faux pas, and, really, nobody present wanted to be in charge of anything. All of us dug and chiseled, scraped and puttered with our toes.

Nobody was going to say, "How about those Rams!" I tried to think of something intelligent to say about the weather, but I clutched. It was just the most uncomfortable three minutes I have spent—above ground, that is, without women present, and fully clothed.

But, Connivin' Ivan arrived after about three awkward minutes, driving an unremarkable pick-up truck. He was a savior. I was glad to see him, and this was not even my problem. All of us wanted some catalytic agent introduced.

The magic of Connivin' Ivan seemed to be centered around his ability to seem non-threatening to anyone. Everybody there immediately felt as if he could whip Ivan: beat him at arm wrestling, a fist fight, a shooting match, a race, a quiz game, cooking—anything. I felt that I could probably take him in any pursuit from obstacle course to mathematical trivia, crossword puzzles to knitting— you name it. I could tell others were saying, "Huh!" And sneering at him. Ivan was small, lightly built, pale, anemic, but unlike the others (except the Mercedes Nerd) actually groomed! He was bespectacled, clean shaven, and dressed for a trip to town—not just our little town, either— more like Harrison or Russellville: a place with traffic lights. But there would be no manhood in attacking him, whipping him, beating him at anything, or besting him in any way. He made me feel like John Wayne, and I can barely make a fist.

Connivin' Ivan sat down at the base of one of Double-Dog's huge oak trees, and we formed a semi-circle facing him. Nobody told us to do that; it just happened. He smiled. I thought I could probably even smile better. Then he spoke.

"Double-Dog, you ride with me, and I drop you out at the main road. Then I go in first, alone. Two minutes later, the rest of you come in: first the Spender Boys with the truck, then you others in one vehicle. The truck goes up to the back door; the other vehicle parks right beside mine, back away from the house. I do all the talking; you guys do all the lifting. If anything goes wrong, don't talk. Let me handle it." Just like that.

We listened, nodded, soaked up all of the instructions perfectly, and, for some reason, did not resent his power. Yes, power! We turned ourselves over to him. A lot of it was because we all understood the delicacy of the operation, but I suppose that each of us felt that he was losing nothing by allowing this diminutive person to run the show. I wanted to get it over with and go home, and so did everybody else, and we suddenly understood each other. It was like being on vacation and having a guide take over and do his job. We just went flaccid and let it happen. Besides, that's the way it's done, apparently.

"Any questions?" asked Connivin' Ivan. I just knew there would be no questions of any kind at all. This group was not in the mood. Wrong again.

"One," said one of the Spender Boys. "Why is the law watchin' us?"

Up on the ridge, high above the mouth of Double-Dog's cave, almost hidden by the dark cedar foliage, the sheriff was plainly visible, now that we had been alerted. He wanted to be seen, and when all of us looked right at him, he lowered his binoculars and disappeared. But he had achieved the wanted effect. The "Big Picture," when it came to knowing Double-Dog Darrell, included the sheriff or one of his deputies in the corner of the frame. No one was going to admit to being intimidated. Nobody answered the question. Nobody had to.

A lot of unspoken, terribly cryptic statements were made in the terseness of Connivin' Ivan's remarks and Double-Dog's mandated silence. We were on the proverbial "need to know" basis, and I had the feeling that if I learned too much I would have to be killed. There were codes, mores, traditions, taboos, protocols. All they wanted from me was a few grunts, and I knew better than to look into the matter any further. We were to move a piano out of enemy territory during a brief, tenuous truce. Period.

&

The Mercedes Nerd and Cowboy John rode with me—all of us in the bench seat of my sissy pick-up truck. I had always thought of the truck in nobler terms, but after I saw what the Spencer Boys drove my vehicle seemed as impotent as I felt. But we followed Connivin' Ivan up through layers of the mountain's geological past exposed along the sorry road where the hill was torn away on the left, and on the right, as always, I noticed the steep drop-off down to other rock slabs and outcroppings many dangerous yards below. (There were refrigerators down there, and old dryers and freezers, and things too rusty to identify.) My truck faltered a little in loose pebbles now and then, but it found traction and climbed pretty well. Behind me I could feel the monster truck of the Spender Boys, eager to give me a shove if I needed it. And, yes, I knew that we were out of order. Up top, I would have to pull over and let the Spender Boys go ahead, as per instructions. They would have to arrive at the Wainwright Compound before me, for sure.

On Smith Mountain, Double-Dog Darrell stood by the side of the dirt road: horseless, wolfless, crowless, and naked-looking—exposed and unprotected. But he was a signal that the compound was about a quarter of a mile away. I waved, out of habit, and Double-Dog grinned and rolled his eyes. This was going to be Spectacle, and he had caused it but was going to miss it. It was the only way. I believe that Old Wainwright could have hit him there with his deer rifle, even though there was a cross-wind. We rolled past Double-Dog and approached Wainwright property.

"Posted," said the first sign; "Keep Out," said another; "No Hunting," then "Do Not Enter"—overkill, really, but clear. And, as if that were not enough, "No Transpassing." When they misspell the sign, they'll shoot! Old law. But we proceeded, with Connivin' Ivan and the Spender Boys running interference. Cowboy John spit into his cup, and the Mercedes Nerd was silent and just tightened his gloves at the wrists. I sat low and gripped the wheel and tried to look casual. In my rearview mirror I saw a white car sliding past Double-Dog on the main road.

The Wainwright dogs had their work cut out for them. The monster truck of the Spencer's had to be barked at, and Ivan's non-descript vehicle needed to be actually bitten. And finally, evidently, it was necessary for them to scratch the sides of my pathetic truck and snarl and claw at the windows all around— two of them actually on board in the back. They wanted to eat my face, I am flattered to say, and the Mercedes Nerd received similar attention on his side. Cowboy John spit. Presently there was a whistle, and the dogs disappeared.

Old Wainwright was one of those mountain men who had initials instead of an actual name. He was R. W. (That is, Are Dubyuh!—with a low raspy growl.) Probably not Robert William, though, because he would have been called Bobby Bill if that had been the case. Anyway, Old Wainwright stepped out on the big porch of the Wainwright Mansion and posed between two cypress pillars (rough hewn), He was standing on one end of a ramp made of unseasoned oak planks. (You learn to recognize things like that on sight very soon after moving into the hardwood forests of the area.) I could tell that the Spender Boys were about to back their truck up to R.W.'s feet and the ramp would be scooted into the truck bed, and it would be a simple matter of rolling the piano up the ramp. Looked like a plan to me. I did not see the necessity for the AR 15 Wainwright was cradling in his arms, but I had seen guns before. Newcomers became aware of guns soon after arrival. Old R.W. would have looked better in a muzzle loader or a 30-40 Craig or a Winchester 76—even a blunderbuss; but he had done Viet Nam. The AR 15 was his security blanket.

It reminded me of when Burl Ives played that bully patriarch in an old western movie: Fat Daddy or something like that—bug-eyed, menacing King-of-the-Mountain sort of fellow.

But soon we were facing the piano itself, in the great room just inside the mansion. I still do not know what the mansion actually looked like. I was preoccupied with dogs. I remember pillars and dogs and a primitive, armed man. And the piano. It was one of those upright beasts made out of steel, cast iron, lead, and what looked like petrified teak—probably stuffed with marble and sand. The Spender Boys immediately grabbed onto one end, lifted, and then dropped to the floor to see how the piano was anchored or glued or bolted down. Then they put their shoulders to the thing like football linemen hitting blocking sleds. The piano did not move. I pitched in, Cowboy John put down his cup, the Mercedes Nerd gripped a handle on the back of the beast, and Old Wainwright, unarmed now, hooked on and grunted. We all grunted! Connivin' Ivan was not about to help; physical labor was not what he was for. The piano sat there and sneered.

"It's awful heavy," said Ma Wainwright. She was hardly inconspicuous in her school bus yellow jogging outfit, but I hadn't seen her at first. She was plicking away at one of those draw poker toys that looks like a calculator. I could hear little bleeps and tweedles as she played on, despite our invasion, over by a huge wood burning stove, all burly and black, but cold now in the summer heat. I know she hit a Full House while we were there. (I was hooked on the thing once myself.)

"We ain't lifted it yet," said Cowboy John, "but I'll bet it is heavy."

I had never thought of that before. If you can't lift it at all, how do you know how heavy it is?

On three, all of us gave it a mighty yank. Then, at Ivan's insistence, we all gave it a yank in one agreed direction. Then we all pushed; then we pulled; then we lifted. It occurred to me that the Mercedes Nerd, the Spender Boys, Cowboy John, and Old Wainwright must really be weak, because I was exerting a great amount of pressure myself and...Never mind.

"Yep. Awful heavy," said Ma Wainwright. Tweedle-de-beep. She sat there like a glob of butternut squash.

"Ain't been moved since that crazy som-bitch left it here," said Old Wainwright. "Shoulda busted it all to hell with a sledge hammer three year ago. Tossed it in Blanco Canyon."

"Damn Double-Dog," muttered Cowboy John.

"Damn straight," said the younger Spender Boy, nodding grimly. Everyone nodded, and a glance went around the site: the glance that said what we all knew once again: Nothing Double-Dog ever touched was uncomplicated. That's why there were stories.

Then The Spender Boys tried lifting, then prying the top plate off the old upright piano. And I was encouraged. It was a wonderful idea. Down inside the hulk, I was ready to believe, Double-Dog had stashed The Lost Confederate Bullion of Booger Hollow—hidden after a Civil War train robbery by guerilla bandits long dead and found by Double-Dog Darrell on one of his moonlit prowlings! Something dramatic like that, for sure! "Hidden for decades" in this ingenious way, this "legendary treasure" would now "re-surface" and cause our "band of misfit adventurers" to kill each other in an "epic confrontation" over the gold and the girl and...Never mind. It was all piano, and the only girl in sight was Ma Wainwright, bleeping and tweedling.

Suddenly, the earth underfoot began to tremble, and there was an uproar in the Wainwright Compound. The "team" rushed out of the mansion to see what was happening. We had become accustomed to the huge military cargo planes that made U-turns in the area, training to fly below radar—but they were gone now, to Afghanistan, probably. Whatever this was, it was on the ground.

The Wainwright dog pack nearly bowled us over in the attempt to get inside the mansion to safety. Howling and yapping, their tails between their legs, they gushed over, under, around, and through our silly crew, and made for the deepest recesses of the back rooms of Wainwright's house. I never saw them again.

There was a reddish brown cloud everywhere outside, and in the middle of it there was the meanest looking truck I had ever seen: a Hummer, all gray and green and terrible, wide and stolid and menacing. A wind blew the dust cloud away, and Moose Vandergrift was standing there like a tree, a tower of sweat and dirt and anger. Immediately, I wanted my mother. Everything endocrine and adrenal left me—fairly spritzed into the void. My knees weakened, my stomach flipped over, and my heart stopped. I had to appreciate Moose's entrance: the skid marks, the anger, the little tornado of dust! Still, I wanted to be elsewhere.

Moose Vandergrift was holding up the biggest pair of filthy overalls in the Ozarks. He wore no shirt, and hair boiled out everywhere: hair like crushed chicken wire, twisted and burnt. His huge eyes were red and his teeth were black, and he wasn't smiling, he was hungry—probably for one of us. I tried to look sour and stringy, but Cowboy John was there ahead of me. The Mercedes Nerd trembled bravely.

I expected Moose to start with "Fee Fie Foe Fum" or something, but I frankly could not understand the sounds that he made. Connivin' Ivan stepped out into the No-Man's Land between our huddle and the bellowing hulk, and immediately he belonged there: the very texture, color, and aura for the scene.

"Glymphlym flgmnr splagem mnart!" roared Moose Vandergrift.

"He says he's angry," Ivan translated.

I knew that. I have an instinct for these things.

Moose roared again, and Connivin' Ivan got the rest of the story. Moose was mad because he had been left out of the operation. Wherever heavy things were moved, it was law that Moose be included. It was a singular insult that he had not been included. By pure chance, he had stopped to investigate Double-Dog's vigil up on the main road, and had learned the sordid truth. One could imagine that Double-Dog had tried to explain, as Connivin' Ivan would now explain, that this was a delicate matter and that Moose was nowhere to be found during the negotiations. Anything.

He was on the job now, Moose was, and everybody should get out of his way. I had no problem with that and slipped behind one of Wainwright's pillars. Moose raged away, and the Spender Boys went into an arm-waving fit, threatening to walk off the job. Cowboy John threw down his spit cup and moved forward. He had ridden Brahma bulls, and he had been a rodeo clown: he had faced beasts many times and was ready now. The

Mercedes Nerd got the other pillar. Testosterone sprayed in all directions. Old Wainwright was unhappy about this uninvited guest, and Connivin' Ivan was temporarily miffed. He looked toward Double -Dog up on the road.

I was thinking about Marlon Perkins on his old wild life TV show. "While Jim wrestles the giant alligator, I will just climb this nearby tree for a better view." Moose was between me and the nearest tree, or I would have climbed one. I looked for hand-holds on the cypress pillar.

The situation was beginning to look just a tad hopeless. But then Connivin' Ivan worked his magic. He backed up against the side of The Spender Boys' ugly truck and slowly slid down—down the side of the cab, slowly, until he was right on the ground, cowering like an old dog that knew he had done something wrong. It was a curiosity: strange. Moose, then the Spender's, then Cowboy John—all went limp: just ceased hostilities. Old Wainwright, too, and in the silence, the Nerd and I gave up our pillars and minced over to the action. All of us formed a semi-circle around Connivin' Ivan's pathetic form. We towered 'round him like so many trees. Ivan looked like something Moose Vandergrift had scraped off his boot. But in two minutes, we were ready to move the piano: all of us, together, as a team. Go figure.

"We are moving a piano," said Ivan quietly. " And when we are finished, everything will be better for everyone. Moose, we were lost and forlorn, but, with you, we are found, and we are mighty. The piano itself would not move without you. It is correct that you are here: it is right, it is necessary, it is good. And it is time." He looked for a nod from Old Wainwright, and got one.

I made a move toward pulling Connivin' Ivan up off the ground, but Moose gently set me aside and stood Ivan on his feet and brushed him off.

Then Moose slapped me on the back and said, "Hrnglcmwr!" And we went into the mansion to get the piano: Me and Moose and the others. It was as if someone had sounded the charge!

Like a stubborn tooth that lets go after a great struggle, the piano yielded to the considerable touch of Moose Vandergrift, and the rest of us. Moose screamed and roared unabashedly with the exertion, and soon all of us bold men were growling and snarling, grunting and straining. Out on the main road, over 400 yards away, Double-Dog actually heard the clamor, and nearly gave up on the project, thinking that the added element of Moose Vandergrift had ruined the chemistry. He wrote sixty-two couplets about it that very night, and I sat through a performance a week later. Even the sheriff, whose curiosity finally got to him, hooked onto the piano at the last second and helped with the final shove into the truck bed. Moose smiled and slapped my back again, and we all laughed with husky, raspy voices. By-God manhood!

Ma Wainwright toted out a big box of sheet music, and the Mercedes Nerd carried the piano stool out to the Spender's truck. Old Wainwright picked up his rifle and looked longingly in the direction of Double-Dog Darrell. He sifted a handful of dust and gaged the windage. It would have been a nice clean shot, too. Pity. The team began to load up, and soon we were all on the road behind the truck that carried the piano that brought us all together. Cowboy John rode with Moose, though, and the Mercedes Nerd and I brought up the rear. Connivin' Ivan hung a left on Highway 123, and I learned later that he was judging a contest at a nearby country church: a face-making/pie supper/chili cook-off benefiting a local charity.

The piano was now in Double-Dog's shanty. Moose and I became friends, but Double-Dog and I had a feud. It would last another two or three months, I knew. (I hated his poem.) I didn't see the Mercedes Nerd or the Spender Boys after the great piano caper, but a week afterwards there was a big rumor going around the hills about Old Wainwright cutting loose with his AR 15 on full automatic, attracting the attention of the sheriff. I knew I would get the whole story later, after my feud with Double-Dog Darrell was over, and I would know when the feud was over when he showed up in my yard—with peanut butter.

That's how it's done.

The Balance of Nature

Advice, whether good or bad, whether solicited or un, disgusts me, makes me sick to my stomach, makes me behave badly. I hate that. Quality people seek and take advice every day. I am apparently too small and too hard-headed. I hate that, and I hate it that I hate that. And it gets worse when I am plainly wrong.

৯

Friend John had always said, "Kill those skunks. No way we can live with skunks. Kill the snakes, too, the poisonous and the non-poisonous. Snakes are evil and they crawl along the ground and they scare the hell out of you. And kill all armadillos, too. They dig up your flower beds, your yard—they're just not worth it. And go out and shoot a deer now and then, too. They're cute, but they'll eat your garden and wreck your orchard. Coons, too: they *will* get into your trash. Opossums are ugly. Just shoot 'em. The deer are carrying Rocky Mountain Spotted Fever, and the birds are carrying the West Nile Virus. Kill 'em all."

Sounds blood-thirsty right away. I had moved out to the hills from a big city, and I thought Bambi and Thumper and all small fuzzy animals were cute. I believed that all things in Nature deserved to live. I had grown up a hunter, but I had decided long ago that what I liked was beef and chicken, ham and bacon, roast pork, and sea food. I did not need to be eating venison or rabbit, and I certainly did not need to be out there killing things for the fun of it. Nor did I join any kook outfits to campaign about Spotted Owls or whales; I figured that snail darters were just going to have to make out the best way they could. I decided that I could not go out where the creatures lived and harm them, for if I had stayed in the city, well off their turf, we would not have the problem. None of them had come into town after me. Fair is fair. Yada yada.

So, Friend John's words fell on deaf ears. I would be what people call "humane." (I don't know if animals call it that, or something else.) John could be my friend, but we would have to agree to disagree on our roles in the great drama of Nature. I would simply have to be shown that John's point of view had merit. Meanwhile, I shunned his advice.

❧

A stray dog came into the yard one day about noon. She was a delicate young white thing: short hair, big eyes, big feet, boundless enthusiasm. She was hungry and covered with ticks and burrs, and she was female: the down side. I turned her in immediately—to Wifey: dragged the woman right out of the kitchen, where she was working on our tomato problem, pointed, and said, "Dog."

"Do not, under any circumstances, speak to that dog," Wifey commanded. "Do not pet her, do not comfort her, do not feed her, do not give her water. Maybe she will go away. I've got enough to do around here with all these tomatoes," Wifey said, and Wifey was fully in charge. (All of our tomatoes had ripened at once.) (One of Nature's laws.)

Within minutes, the dog was being combed and groomed, pampered and fed and watered, de-ticked and de-loused, and bathed, by Wifey. She had been a nurse too long. Out in the woods later, I smirked; behind Wifey's back, I chuckled silently; while she was tied up on the phone that afternoon, I did a little touchdown dance, out behind the barn; down in the tomato patch, harvesting still more, I did a great impersonation of Wifey. I was not seen, and I got away with all of it. The surplus tomato problem would have to wait. It was time for the dog drill.

The precious bundle had probably been dumped off by someone from a city—out along Highway 7—like a hundred others before her. Country folks are supposed to gather up all these animals and adopt them, fall in love with their helpless eyes, fight fleas and ticks and burrs and infections, and get the dogs healthy enough to go back out on the highway and become road pizza. Someone thinks that is fair. The tourists come along and nail them with their cars, and the vultures get a feast. (That's part of the Balance of Nature, too, according to John.) Always, categorically always, we responded. Humans are part of Nature, too. We could not say no to the dogs—any of them.

Besides, "You don't shoot the dogs," Friend John had declared. "Dogs are noble beasts: Man's Best Friend. You'll go straight to hell if you shoot a dog."

One more time, then, Wifey put another dog through the proverbial pit stop. I helped with the bathing and some of the tick removal, but it was mainly Wifey's doing. We had been there and done that many times before. One dog had been snake bitten; another had been led out onto the highway by a dog we were actually trying to keep as a pet; others had broken away when we had confined them, and we saw the buzzards circling just down the highway. This little gal would probably be a variation on the theme; but in exactly what respect, we could not know. We worked, trying not to love the dog.

She seemed to want to lie on the back deck where it was cool and a good breeze could hit her and she was up off the ground. For a pup, she was very ladylike. I put dignified words into her mouth, and Wifey gave her baby talk, and that first meeting was warm and satisfying. That night, she was our guest. She seemed grateful for the food, especially grateful for the personal attention, and at peace following her ordeal of being lost or abandoned. She liked her blanket. She had found safety, and she seemed capable of enjoying it.

At about 2 a.m. I heard her bark a little, but that all died down, and I suspected that she had greeted a possum or a coon or a deer. "We won't be seeing any more animals for a while," I mumbled, and went back to sleep. She was already becoming territorial. At about 5 a.m., I heard a real ruckus outside, and I could tell that the dog had encountered another of Nature's people. She was taking care of the place—on guard. Noble beast. I went back to sleep, trusting the dog, and God, and Nature.

∽

It was cool on the mountain that night, and we had the windows open. When I opened my eyes at dawn, I knew something was wrong. I have an instinct about these things. I sensed trouble. I sensed that the dog had barked at a skunk, right there on the back deck, and had been fired upon. The stench was crippling. The dog was standing there in the back yard, helpless and hopeless, and reeking.

We had been wondering how long the dog would remain clean when we bathed her. Now we knew. We had also wondered what we were ever going to do with all our tomatoes, which were ripening by the hundreds. So, we used the juice of the tomatoes to clean up the dog (well-known remedy), she got loose following the invasive bath, and she ran out on the highway. While chasing her, I noticed that one of our fruit trees had lost most of its bark to a deer—probably rubbing the velvet off its antlers. But I was falling down at the time, because I had stepped into a hole dug there by an armadillo, so I had other problems. I fully expected to be bitten by a rattlesnake at any moment or by a mosquito that had visited a deer or a bird. I could see where it was all leading.

We were able to dump the bath water into the tomato patch both times, recycling the water, and the seeds from the second batch (all that fresh tomato juice) would probably germinate there and become the next garden. I caught the dog before Highway 7 splattered her, and Wifey arranged for an adoption—far off the highway, back in the hills, with a couple she had met at church: just phone-whipped that puppy right there! When we delivered the dog, the dog vomited in the car; but we received peaches and some cucumbers from those nice folks. The Balance of Nature.

I got a shot at a coon that very night. Well, I fired over its head with some relatively harmless rat shot. It had called for the food that we put on the upper deck for our feral cats—the only "pets" we seemed to be allowed. Two days later, about the time the skunk smell was dissipating on our mountain, the vultures were circling out near our mail box on the highway. A raccoon had crossed over, crossing over.

"If you don't shoot 'em, " John had said, "they'll get it another way, but you will be damaged. It ain't purty, but that's the way it goes. It's the Balance of Nature. Nothin' you can do about it. Remember: there are bears out there, and mountain lions hunting all those cute fuzzy animals in your yard."

I was changed by all of this, of course. Now I wanted to save the trees so that the creatures would have a place to hide; I wanted cleaner air because I had smelled the skunk's work, up close and personal; I wanted to grow our own food, because it's noble; I wanted to be compassionate to Nature's creatures—to live and let live—because I was suddenly afraid.

I learned that I loved country life. Really. We were part of The Balance of Nature: Wifey and me, and Scenic Byway Seven.

The Hiker's Ashes

We had been warned: the local "authorities" are not to be trusted. "They had a suicide here a while back," we were told. "It was a man who shot himself three times in the back, tied cement blocks to his feet, and flung himself off a cliff into a lake. Somewhere in there he managed to cut his own throat, too."

All of that had ostensibly happened before Wifey and I had moved out of the violent city and into the peace and quiet of the Ozark hills. We listened to the stories because they were colorful and we were bored. Also, we liked the neighbor lady, who had the lovely collection of suspicions and shared them so generously.

"They have mysterious fires around here, too. The big bed & breakfast that was on Green Mountain was one of them. It closed for lack of business, then it was up for sale for a few years, then it sat there for a few years gathering spider webs and critters. All gas and electric were cut off, of course, and nobody went near the place. But it was insured, and one night it went up in flames. Paper said it was being investigated, but there was no follow-up."

Hmmm.

But that was probably just another of the fascinating tales the neighbor lady had in her quiver, we reasoned. She was a woman beset with tormentors. On her television set, the weather was always better on Channel 10 than on Channel 3: more rain and better temperatures. Bears and mountain lions frequented her backyard and made outdoor activities impossible after dark. Her government lied to her about everything—and that meant local, state and national government. She could tell when the phone rang who was after her money and why, so she knew when not to answer the phone. And she kept an eye on Scenic Highway Seven, because there were some bad people coming through on that highway. The eighteen-wheelers always let their engines and jake brakes blat right by her house. The neighbor lady had quite a list.

"There's a bottomless pit out there, too." Ah yes, the old bottomless pit routine. "People disappear. They simply disappear—evaporate!"

"Maybe that guy who committed suicide just couldn't make it to the bottomless pit after he killed himself and had to go to the lake!" I teased the neighbor lady sometimes.

"Scoff if you will. There's a bottomless pit out there, and people disappear. Period."

❧

That one became tiresome after a while. Nobody was able to name anybody who had disappeared, and it was not difficult to imagine someone pulling up stakes and moving away, completely and suddenly, in the dead of night, not looking left or right (or back). We had met locals who had done that and returned later after finding the greater world wanting. Young people disappeared right after graduation from high school; some disappeared after falling out of love; some went broke after trying yet another antique shop venture in town or along the highway, and then "disappeared." Or escaped.

"They're in on it together: all of Them." (I knew about Them—the Big THEM: the ones who have their feet in our faces, keeping us down.) "They dispose of people—and places, too. There was a house that burnt up 200 yards from the EMT/ Ambulance barn; there was another one that burnt just two miles from the firehouse—only one stop sign in between. And there was that big restaurant that was hit by heat lightning in February while its owners were away on vacation—after it had been up for sale for several years."

We grew weary of it. It was a local joke that when things

didn't work out, you just lit a match and the insurance company took the fall—according to the neighbor lady. As if insurance companies had no investigators. We listened to her entirely too much. It was just gossip, probably. No way it could be out in the open like that and go undetected. Probably. Her stories became humorous to us. We were secretly above all of that mundane pettiness.

Still, whenever there was a fire, Wifey and I observed, the structure went down, right into the basement, a fully-consumed pile of ashes and melted metal and cooked masonry. Very thorough process. And it usually happened at night.

The volunteer fire departments were good at rescues, from all evidence. The high angle rescue squad was proud and proficient. (They were all about retrieving dangling people: people who got half-way up or down cliffs.) We were not an area ravaged by forest fires, so the forestry people were good at their jobs, apparently. The First Responders were heroic and efficient. They were able to upright stricken trucks, disentangle ensnared drivers, pry open the bent-up vehicles that routinely bounded off the sharp mountain curves, and free the victims. Down on the river, when canoeists needed a bale-out, the locals were fast and effective. I pointed all of that out to the neighbor lady—as a new-comer, just quietly observing.

"Ever see a building half-burned? Ever see a fire they put out?"

"Well. I read about a barn they saved after only three bales of hay burned..."

"They saved that one because it was not scheduled to burn! Do you think it would have been saved if it had been a failed business place? I think not! They're all in it together. When a building has to go, it goes, and it goes completely."

"Well, really, it looks like it would be just about impossible for the volunteer firemen to get to a fire over these terrible roads, at some of these remote locations—especially at night—in winter, for God's sake, or in a heavy rain when the low-water bridges are impassable. And they get heart attack victims out of some of the damnedest places imaginable, and transport them to the hospital and save their lives. It happens all the time."

"They burn up what needs to be burnt up, and they save what needs to be saved." The neighbor lady was adamant. And she was capable of postures and attitudes that pulled people into all the fine conspiracies.

Wifey and I decided not to talk about it at all. From our lips, tales like that could sound vicious. We would not want to make enemies of people who knew where we lived. We decided we could live out our lives without ever besmirching the honor of volunteer firemen and rescue workers and people who answer the call when there is trouble.

In the city, when there was a slum that needed to be cleared, someone built a stadium and a huge parking area in that neighborhood; when an apartment complex was twenty-five years old, its upkeep was abandoned, riff-raff was moved in, and ten years later it burned. There was a little consensual smile in the community. It was almost natural! There was "conventional suspicion," but no real proof that anybody ever pressed.

We almost approved, by doing nothing, by saying nothing. It was just property. "The greater good," and all that. In our new home in the hills, we could smile and move along and play the game, if necessary. Of course, maybe there was no game being played. Maybe there are just cycles—chains of events—rather than modus operandi.

"Remember the bootlegging," the neighbor lady kept saying. Oh yes, we knew about the bootlegging. "And when that armored car went off the road and spilled all that money, don't you tell me they got all that money back! I'll bet whole bags of that money got away from them."

"'Paper said they got it all back and were proud of the honesty of the locals," I told her.

"If you believe that, you believe that the auctions are all honest!"

"The auctions?" said Wifey, jolted into the middle of the conversation by something she really cared about. "What's wrong with the auctions?"

"I wouldn't get all that specific," the neighbor lady said, with her eyes bulging, "but sometimes the bidding is over before everybody knows what's being sold, and somebody who knows the auctioneer particularly well gets a good deal."

"Everybody knows the auctioneer," I said.

"Live in your dream world if you like. There's a lot going on around here that you know nothing about."

"Sounds like we don't want to know some of these things," Wifey told the neighbor lady.

"I know things that would make your blood run cold," she said. And when she said things like that, I knew she was leaving momentarily, and I would not have to get my shins kicked black and blue under the table as I pumped the neighbor lady for more of this vicious gossip that I was simply above.

A young hiker's ashes were discovered one morning in the ruins of a former crafts shop on one of the highest ridges in the county, right along Scenic Highway Seven, just a few miles from our retreat. Not much was left of him, from all accounts: ashes, a bone or two, part of a backpack, earrings, a tongue rivet, like that.

When I learned of it, I just knew that somebody had been unable to transport the fresh-killed stranger to the bottomless pit a few mountains over (where he naturally belonged) and had been forced to incinerate the abandoned building to get rid of him. Or, maybe the entire platoon of local emergency workers had conspired to burn up yet another piece of property, as the neighbor lady would have it, and failed to notice the hapless hiker asleep in the targeted building. Or, perhaps he had crawled in there to get out of the elements and the whole thing was spontaneous human combustion. Or, a meteorite or an asteroid or a bolt of lightning might have done him in. The neighbor lady was my mentor by then.

Anyway, according to the local newspaper, an investigation was warranted. The body had to be identified, and the mystery of the death had to be solved. The sheriff and his deputies were feverishly at work clearing it up at press time. Weekly newspaper. (These things happen with weekly newspapers. A one-week interruption can occur right in the middle of a scoop.)

The following week, since everybody already knew the outcome of the investigation, the headlines in the paper screamed, "Hanson Named Goat Wormer of the Year." In a related story, the rumor that a flashing yellow light would be installed at The Junction was officially debunked. On Page Two, the county fair was deemed a major success. Mary Davidshoffer had won a quilt at the rodeo. No story, even a buried one, had anything to do with the hiker or his plight.

The neighbor lady, however, because she had her fingers on the pulse of the place, filled us in on the details. "The High Sheriff determined that the young man died of mysterious causes, and that the building burnt because some oily rags heated up in a ray of sunshine."

"Well, was the building insured?"

"Nope. Not this time. And you know what that means."

"What does that mean?"

"Somebody murdered that hiker and tried to burn up the body. Any fool could see that. If there's insurance, it's arson; if there's no insurance, it's to cover up something more serious. Look for dope and money now."

"Any chance it was just a kid who needed to get under a roof and had a cooking fire get away from him while he slept?" (I had a flare for quick fiction myself.)

"Not a chance. There are no accidents. We know all we're ever going to know about it, too. Unless that kid was connected somewhere and big people are involved, it's all a bunch of ashes, and that's all there is to it."

❧

About two months later, a new sheriff was elected. The entire scene of the "crime" was chiseled out of the ground so that the State Boys could park their vehicles and work on the new stretch of asphalt paving. All the stories died away. Earth spun on its axis and rotated around the sun, and life went on. The neighbor lady found out that the hiker's remains went to a small town in Tennessee. Fed Ex.

"You want to know more, you can go down to the courthouse and ask questions. You'll have quite a wait, though, because those young women down there are always out in the yard smoking."

I cannot even take you to the supposed spot where the alleged "murder" might possibly have occurred, maybe. I think perhaps it slid off into the canyon sometime last winter. We have other things than gossip to do around here anyway. I just won't talk about it any more.

Everything's at Scenic Point

Between home and town, at the highest point around, there is a popular tourist spot called simply Scenic Point. You can get off the highway there and gird your loins for the dive down into the town, or you can rest up after the climb—depending on which way you are going. Sometimes in the morning, it is possible to imagine an angel stepping off one of the clouds to mingle with the tourists. From Scenic Point you can see for miles on a clear day while waiting out an eighteen wheeler or logging truck, perhaps—or just meditating a little—or planning your next move. Or just teetering on the brink.

I would stop there occasionally to pose as a tourist, check out license plates, and hobnob with passers-through, asking how things were going in Minnesota or Iowa or Nebraska or Texas (places I cared a lot about), and sharing the pleasures of The View with people from places I was curious about. When you see a Hawaiian license place in mid-America, you wonder: put together a little back story for the car, etc. At Scenic Point I would hear accents and see clothes and faces and shades of skin that refreshed my spirit. I was connected.

Once I noticed a young California couple standing silently, just gazing off into the valley. Almost straight down, there was the beautiful pastureland among the trees and roads; then further out, the whole range of mountains and hills, all green at that time. The kids were just stopped by it: transfixed. I said nothing, but I was curious about their silence and got close to them, pretending to be similarly distracted, rapt, and absorbed. (Indeed, I was not immune.) After four or five minutes, the two of them nodded, disengaged as if the whole scene had been switched off by someone with a TV remote, and turned away. Then they stopped and turned back toward the view, and the boy said, framing the scene with his hands, "I get it." The girl said, "Me, too." They gave each other "high fives," got into their California car, and drove off to the South.

Sometimes I would do my little sidling act, edging over toward a little cluster of tourists like some twisted stalker or the neighborhood creep, and I would eavesdrop. There would be some gasping and the mandatory ooos and ahhhs, but often there was the expressive silence of people thinking deep thoughts. It seems to happen when there is an abyss at your feet.

That was normal at Scenic Point. Everyone had to have a registration of the impact—a picture of some kind, and there was a souvenir shop open most of the time for those who just thought it was all very pretty: coke machines, a little fudge, some crafty items. Touristy place. But for me it was a reminder that the whole world was still out there, and that people are pretty much the same everywhere, for all their differences. I had not left Earth. The place was therapy; it was CNN, it was re-supply, contact.

꙳

One day I was there transfusing myself once again, and a stranger approached me. (Who else would he be?) "Pretty view," he said.

"Yes. I enjoy it often."

"Which way you headed?" he asked.

"Oh, I live here," I confessed. "Coupla miles away."

"Good. Wise decision."

"I think so."

"I mean, I've been that way," he said, pointing North, " and there's nothing—and I've been that way," he said, pointing the opposite direction, "and nothing's there, either."

He really had my attention now, and I looked him over. Cotton and polyester, nondescript, touristy pastel, medium everything, even to his skin tone. Hell, I was talking to Everyman. His accent was North American, touches of everything and everywhere, like mine.

"Nothing there, huh?"

"Nothing. I meet people in traffic, and I think, 'Where in the hell are you going? I've been back this way, and there's nothing!' Why do they bother to go on?"

"Well," I offered, "What must they think, meeting you—headed in the direction they're coming from? I mean, they have been where you're going—just as you have been where they're going..."

"But I keep thinking there must be something somewhere—back where they came from, because so many are coming down that road. I know what I know, and I want to turn them back. They are wasting their time. You see what I'm getting at here?"

"Yeah, but they're searchers, too. They want confirmation."

"But they're heading toward nothing! And nobody seems to stop them."

Well, I diagnosed him immediately and decided to grunt and walk away. I was not in the mood to get into what "nothing" was or what "something" might be—to him! I wanted out of the conversation, stat!

But then I noticed the tower. They had a wooden tower up at Scenic Point that would get you about thirty more feet of elevation if you climbed it. There, at the highest point in the hills, someone built a tower to get a few feet higher. You could go up there and dangle your toes over the side and think even deeper thoughts. Something terribly significant about that. Perfect.

"Why don't you climb up there?" I suggested. "You can see more from there. I've always thought they built that tower for people who get all the way up here and can't believe that is all there is."

"I've been up," he said, "and I took a good look, too. Nothing North, nothing South.

"Nothing." (Well, I was drawing a blank, for sure.)

"Nothing there." He stared into the view, and so did I. "Nothing anywhere."

How to get loose? I needed to drop something on this guy and get home to my wife. It had to be deep, and it had to be deep quick. I had had enough of Scenic Point for the day.

"Well, I guess all of it is right here, then, huh?" I said cautiously. "All of it—right where we stand."

He looked at me as if I had hit upon something profound. I was willing for that to be the case. I even got to thinking about it myself. And when you take yourself seriously, you're in trouble.

"I guess you're right: everything must be right here." He stared into space.

"Well," I said, after the appropriate pause, "I leave it to you. I've got to get home and mulch the raspberry patch. Take care." And I left him there, gazing.

But as I walked away, he said, "Thank you." I waved but did not look back.

And I imagined that someday he would write a penetrating book that I did not understand, and mention this enigmatic, ancient traveler he had encountered along Life's highway, who had said things that made all the difference. I tried to put all that into my walk—to imagine him looking at me as I walked away, an "image etched into his mind forever" sort of thing, a venerable sage returning to his humble life.

Yeah, right. I didn't go back there until I was sure he was long gone. There was never a report that he had jumped off the cliff or anything. He must have sallied forth and headed toward Nothing, reluctantly leaving Everything behind. I know that he did not take Everything with him, because it was all still there when I last checked. Imagine a lonesome, whispering wind, fading.

A Necessary Mind

His voice was sounding like gears grinding, his forehead was crusted and caked where it was not raw, and his face was wind-burned—all red under the white stubble, but Old Clem was indoors, at least, and it was a relief to those of us who cared. His sheepskin coat was draped over his chair, and his winter cap was parked by his plate. He had come in for some hot food. His hands were chapped and wrinkled and discolored, and they looked like they had been chiseled out of the face of a cliff. The hands made the Senior Center's flatware look like something stolen from The White House.

"I moved out of those apartments because I felt that I was losing my awareness," he said with great effort, and some volume. He was having to force his words through a junkyard of a throat, and they bounced around over the table like busted rocks. "It was too nice. All my problems were over. Food, clothing, shelter, heat, light, amusement, companionship, bathroom—all of it was wired. I was rotting there."

"But isn't that what people want?" someone asked, as others were drawn in.

"Not me," he rattled and clattered. "I went there because it was what I thought I wanted, all right, but it turned out that all of my problems were solved for me. Problem solving was taken away from me, and man is a problem solving creature. I was becoming a potted plant."

Old Clem was having the steak fingers, and he had one of them in his hand now to gesture with. "A man has to think. I was losing track of the seasons! Winter, Summer, Spring, Fall—it was all the same in my apartment: 74 degrees, whether it took air conditioning or heat to keep it there! Always gloomy, never sunny, never really cloudy, never windy, no rain, no snow. It was always the same way in my apartment, and I didn't have to leave if I didn't want to."

It was not exactly an assisted living facility that Clem had occupied, but it was perfect for a Senior Citizen. Wifey and I had, in fact met him at those apartments a few years earlier when her mother had lived there in her last days. It was a nice place for a sweet little old lady who liked picture puzzles, quilts, lace, Lawrence Welk, Jesus, and a half acre of glass figurines. It was warm, it was secure, it was complete—friends right outside your door, all in your own age and income group: no stairs, no cares, no pairs—strictly Senior Adult Singles. But, yeah, all of your problems would be a phone call away from solution.

"I took a shower every day and forgot what I actually smelled like. Everywhere I walked was level, boring. I could get away with making mistakes. I cooked at first, but then I got too lazy and started eating frozen dinners. I got so hooked on TV that I would watch people curse and have fist fights! My brain was dying."

"Well, were people bothering you—invading your space— trying to make you do things you didn't want to do?" I asked. I had read too many stories.

"No, that wasn't it. It was the awareness thing. With your mind, it's 'use it or lose it,' and my mind wasn't necessary over there. I got me a trailer, and I live down on the creek a mile off the tar. When the leaves turn red and gold, I'm in the middle of that; when it's cold, I'm figurin' out how to get warm; when it's hot, I set my feet in that creek, and I am in touch with the Universe. That water flows over my feet, down to the river, and ultimately into the sea."

"Awareness restored," I ventured.

"Yes!" he bellowed, pointing a steak finger at me. "When the wind shifts out of the South to the Northeast, I pick up on that! When there are more or less acorns or walnuts, I know about it. I'm plugged in again. I contemplate the mysteries of the blossoms." I noticed his hands trembling a bit, and he gave off the vague impression that dry parts of him could fall off—that chips from his cracked and crazed flesh could simply drop away. But first, broken chunks of his throat just had to be flying around—with sparks! His throat—probably his whole body—needed medical attention, stat!

"Looks like Nature's roughed you up pretty good," said White Pony Tail, one of the pool players.

"I'm just fine," the voice rasped, then broke, then crashed into a strangled cough.

"Oh, yeah—you're just fine."

The lady in charge of the Center was nearby and could not help but notice Old Clem and his condition. She had no authority to reel him in and force any kind of medical anything on him. He lived independently, after all, and his awareness was "just fine." He had not "surrendered" to the Center—he was a "guest"—so she had no papers telling her of his Next of Kin. ("Next of Kin" seems to get into everything you sign up for after a certain age.)

"You ought to have that throat looked at, Clem," she said. "It sounds terrible. At least get yourself some over-the-counter stuff."

"I'm just fine. It's been like this for a month, and I'm still goin' strong." And he ate vigorously. "Anyway, I'm not rotting away in front of a TV set, all propped up on pillows. I've got my wood stove; I've got my books; I've got things to think about."

"You've got walking pneumonia," said Wifey. Wifey was a nurse for many years, and she knew what she was talking about.

Old Clem looked around now, and he could see that about six people were paying close attention to him. He had his awareness, all right, and he was aware of the concern—the alarm, really—on all of the faces in view. He looked just a little trapped, and I half-way expected him to jump up and run off to pout—to become angry and cantankerous like old men are supposed to—and tell us all to mind our own business. In every movie and book that I knew about, old guys like this did not simply roll over—they went further into denial and ran off into the woods and died.

But Old Clem looked at each of us, quite deliberately, and then at all of us with quick, darting glances. He took a drink of his hot tea and broke things loose a little in his terrible throat. "You guys really think I should go over and have the clinic take a look at me?"

There was a chorus of "Oh, yeah" and "The sooner the better" and "Really, Clem, go over there today" and "Have Doc scope it out"—everybody at once. White Pony Tail told him that his voice sounded like jake brakes—things truckers know about. Clem's crusted eyebrows arched in surprise at the swiftness and the unanimity of the response, and he nodded, and then he smiled.

"I guess I better get me a bath. They never stop with just looking down your throat."

"You'd be surprised where they never stop looking," said the In Charge lady, and all the women in the little gang nodded knowingly. There was chuckling, then quiet laughter all around.

ৡ

Old Clem didn't die. At least, he didn't die just then. And nobody went out and made him stop living in his trailer out by the creek. But he did make certain changes in his lifestyle. He turned himself in, signed up at the Center, and became a "necessary mind" at lunch. He was thinking some deep thoughts out there in the woods, and he decided that he could share them with the lunch mob in town. Maybe we couldn't keep up with him, but to us, Old Clem was a keeper.

You've Got to be Careful

Y ou go down some of these dirt roads," the neighbor lady
warned, "and you might not come back. People have
disappeared. There are things to be seen, way back off
the highway in the wilderness areas, that folks don't want seen.
You've got to be careful where you go and who you trust."

Our guru and confidante and spiritual advisor when we
began our retirement in the hills was our neighbor, a small
round lady who always had alarming and intriguing things to
tell us. She advised us on where to shop, who was who, what
was what, and, of course, the weather. Thanks to her, we always
knew what was going to happen during upcoming seasons, no
matter what the addled weathermen on TV had to say. And,
thanks to her, we knew secrets, we had insider information, and
we had a social roadmap.

"There are poachers in these hills," she warned us, "and
there are meth labs. And there are people growing pot. There
are stills, too—just like in the old movies. People are up to
things, and they don't want surprises. And they've got guns."

Well, we hadn't met anybody but "nice folks," as far as we
knew. We seemed to be surrounded by warm, friendly people—
like the neighbor lady herself—and we did not feel particularly
threatened. The back roads were spooky, all right, but mainly
because of their roughness. If your car gave out, you were in
trouble. But we had yet to be shot at or abused in any way by
the locals.

"There's a bottomless pit out South there between a coupla

mountains, and they say it's got bodies in it. People disappear."
The neighbor lady's eyes would get big during such reports.

"Bottomless pit?" I had to ask. "How do they figure that?"

"It's a deep hole, and you throw a rock down there and it don't hit anything. You never hear it hit. Of course, nobody's ever gone down it to find out."

"How do they know there are bodies down there?"

"It's just one of the old stories. I can live the rest of my days without ever going near that place. You'd be well advised..."

"Oh, don't worry about us! Bottomless pits we don't need." Indeed, I had no intentions of going near any pits, bottomless or otherwise. And if there were bodies, Wifey would have me re-arranging them in tasteful configurations. She might even call the cops. That, too, could be a mistake.

"You could make a wrong turn, you know—end up in somebody's yard out there—get set upon by a pack of dogs—get shot with some old squirrel gun—and dumped into a bottomless pit."

❦

In those early moments of our sojourn in the hills, Wifey and I listened carefully to everything anybody told us; and so, for a while, we looked down those old dirt roads until they bent off into the forest, and kept steadfastly to the high roads! I had no intentions of getting my Dakota pick-up unnecessarily dirty or scratched up or bottomed-out! We learned about low-water bridges—fords, actually, where you crossed streams and rivers when the water was low. I resolved never to do that, because I could see myself calling some hillbilly tow truck to drag my truck out of a river, and being the butt of cracker barrel jokes forever. I would not tempt fate. Also, I could imagine my poor pick-up flying to pieces in some of the rough spots.

Within a few weeks, however, we dove off the main highway into the abyss, left or right, with amazing confidence. We explored; we got lost and found ourselves again; we experimented—pushing the proverbial envelope. We crept along ledges, past the mouths of caves, through the dark forests, over, under, around, and through all of it. We became fearless. (Well, all right: Wifey became fearless and dragged me along on such forays. I would rather have read a good book.) And somewhere along the way we decided that we had to see the bottomless pit someday, if for no other reason, just to have a place to dump bodies if the occasion ever arose. You never know.

"You've gotta know the back roads," the neighbor lady had told us. "Just don't go there. Those are the rules."

"How can we do that? Suppose we suddenly have a whole mess of bodies to get rid of. What if we haven't been to the bottomless pit locale by then? What will we do? Ask the neighbors? To know the back roads, we have to drive the back roads, don't we?"

"You can joke about it if you want to, Smarty Pants, but mark my words..."

She had warned us about panthers, and we had seen no panthers; she had warned us about bears, and we had seen no bears; she had warned us about strange weather, but no weather is strange to the Ozarks. She had stood vigil in her back yard when the terrorists attacked our country, ready to fight off errant al-Qaeda scum. None showed up on our mountain. Things remained peaceful. Still, we heeded every warning, and I was armed to the teeth at all times. If only one bad dream comes true, that is enough.

We were trying to find a tiny church tucked away in a hollow far off any pavement, down a terrible little road that seemed to file off to a point in the wilderness. And it was getting dark. It was autumn, and in places the road disappeared amid fallen leaves. The beauty all around us soaked up my half-hearted anger. There was a pie supper out there (benefiting the cemetery fund), and Wifey and I needed to be there, for a reason which now escapes me. Why it was at night was unclear to me also. But adventure loomed, and so there we were: Wifey, me, and two sweet little old ladies with blue hair and chains on their glasses. One was my mother-in-law and the other was the neighbor lady Herself!

"Are you absolutely sure about this, Dear?" I moaned.

"We will find it, and it will be fun," she told me. I believed her.

"Remember that bottomless pit?" said the neighbor lady, "I think it's around here close, down one of these side roads."

"There are no side roads," said my mother-in-law. "This IS the side road. Anything to the side of this is an animal trail."

"You got that right, Madame," I said. (I always called my mother-in-law Madame: a peremptory strike.)

"It would be a driveway, actually. And remember what I told you about suddenly appearing in someone's yard unannounced and uninvited," comforted the neighbor lady, trembling a little.

Wifey, who was at the wheel on almost all of these plunges off the pavement, immediately turned and began following a grassy strip, wagon ruts, stony shelves crossing low streams covered in yellow leaves, an array of "No Hunting" signs, and low-slung vines above a darkening tunnel through the trees! I could tell she was happy.

"We are doomed," said the neighbor lady.

"That does not mean we are bad people," I said.

Wifey cut loose with a high-pitched, maniacal cackle, and drove on, bouncing merrily with all aboard.

"There are hillbillies around here—real ones. We are not wanted here," warned the neighbor lady. She looked small and helpless, like Madame. And me.

"Just gotta ask a few questions. These people can probably tell us where the church is. They live here." Wifey pushed the Dakota hard.

"They might come out shooting. Stop the car. This is a mistake."

It was too late. We popped suddenly into a clearing, and in front of us there loomed an old rusty pick-up—not a Dakota, either: no extended cab or anything. It was the mandatory

Ozark lawn ornament. And it was just draped with some of the crudest-looking people I had ever seen. And, yes, they were armed. Camouflage outfits all around. There was only one dog, though: a trembling, rodent-looking thing.

The children ran out and surrounded our vehicle, giggling and screeching and jumping up and down. I could see that their camouflage outfits were new, and they wore rugged little boots. A lady, rather slim and ruddy, was wiping her hands on a towel and coming out of the old house, brushing away a falling leaf. The guy with the gun stood his weapon against the old truck and trotted over to the Dakota.

"You folks lost?"

"Yes," said Wifey. "There's a pie supper out here somewhere, and we can't find the church."

The neighbor lady began to pray, and so did Madame—to two different gods, no doubt—one a Catholic version, one a Baptist. I was busy assessing the situation and looking for an escape route

"Well, I can't tell you how to get there," the man said, "but I can take you there. If I tried to tell you, you could get really lost and end up over at the bottomless pit or somewhere worse."

"Worse?" I asked.

"Tell you what. We were about to leave for the pie supper ourselves. All you have to do is follow us. Then, when it's over, we'll put you with someone who'll get you back to town. How's that?"

"Sounds like a plan," said Wifey.

While I was looking around for an escape route, I spotted a teenaged boy slipping around the side of the house. I noticed that the house had been stripped for a paint job, and there were signs that brush had been cleared out of the yard recently. There was some new siding under a window, and a whole new window beside that. Obvious renovations were going on. Then the boy emerged from the back of the house, driving a Jeep Cherokee not more than a year old.

"You folks look kinda cramped in there," said the

gentleman. "One of you wanna ride with us? We've got plenty of room. I'm Jim, and this is Marcie."

"You folks want something to drink? I've brewed up some sun tea," said the lady of the house. "You look a little parched."

"No, thank you," I said for all of us. "It's just terror. We hate being lost."

"Well, you are lost no more!" said the gentleman. "Let's get loaded up and go to that church. We just got here ourselves this summer. Came up outa Dallas. But I love these little pie suppers, don't you? They are so quaint."

I rode with Jim and the kids (and we had some chips!), and Marcie got in with Wifey and the ladies, and we went to the pie supper. We knew half of the people there, and met a few of the others. Wifey ended up buying two pies, but the prices got up too high for our wallets after that. No shots were fired. But Jim told me one thing on the way that made me chuckle a little. "You gotta be careful out here. Some of these people are dangerous. There's a bottomless pit near here..."

Resident Cynic

During one of the times when we were talking to each other, I caught Double-Dog Darrell at the critical moment that Old Mr. Hooper, a sane local friend, used to call "betwixt and between"—an unfortunate interlude between the last medical dosage that could make Darrell personable and the next check that could make him solvent. It was a time when he was not getting the medication (or whatever) necessary to keep him pleasant and lovable.

"Critical" was, in fact, the operative word, because at such times Double-Dog could lash out at you and turn your mind inside out, tear your id to pieces, and fill you with such self-doubt that you were arguably poisoned. And there was always the thought that, last winter, he had dropped by and written his name in the snow—his whole name, the accepted way! And his last name was Dangerfield. (He later told me that he did it with a one-gallon squeeze bottle. Zany guy.)

I was down in the woods on an autumn day, sitting on a rock, thinking deep thoughts, and secretly thanking Wifey for taking me out of the city to this beautiful place, wondering if I had thanked her face-to-face recently. And he was suddenly there.

"Thinkin' about it, huh?" he blurted, standing right behind me. I leaped into the air. He was all dressed up like an old prospector, right down to the rock hammer and the pan. He was not as impressive on the ground as on horseback, but he was still tall, wiry, and very much at home out there in the rocks and trees. And today he had a patch over one eye—an adornment. He was not armed, but that made no difference. I was. (It was back when I thought I should be armed when I was in the woods.)

"My God, Darrell, I hate it when you do that!"

"Do what?"

"Creep up on me like that."

Then I noticed that he had his four wolves with him, and his goat. His crow was on his shoulder as usual. I guess I wasn't being quite alert.

"I was just reading your mind," he started in. "You had flung aside your obsession with The Bottomless Pit, and you were sittin' here contemplating the 'shrinking wilderness' concept, and how we should 'save the trees' and halt 'urban sprawl' and how Presumptuous Man is destroying Nature. You came out here from the city as if someone was watchin' you—like you were important enough to be missed, like you mattered and had influence and could make a difference." All of this was unprovoked.

"Actually, I was thinking about a great little Chinese buffet..."

"Statistically, the coasts and the cities are where things are happening, and the population has abandoned and is daily fleeing the hinterlands to stack up and jam together along the seashores and along certain corridors inside the continent. Bambi and Thumper, as you call them, have had to go into town. The coyotes are living in L.A., and raccoons and possums and bears have become social creatures underfoot. There was good footage of a moose in an urban swimming pool. Everybody else is going into the cities, and so are the critters! So, you're thinking that the cities are coming after the Wilderness, threatening Nature itself! To you it's a tragedy, an emergency, possibly a catastrophe!"

"Look, Darrell..."

"Where you live now, the endangered species is Man! The Wilderness is encroaching, not shrinking." I hadn't thought of that, and I didn't want to.

"Okay, you win. I was really thinking about getting old."

"You're new at being old, and you're not *old* old yet at all, but you have become a Senior Citizen, and that seems to mean that you have lived long enough to encounter a few gross misconceptions that you used to consider knowledge. Enjoy. It is a humbling experience. It is, more accurately, an apparently endless series of humbling experiences, like adolescence—or marriage!"

"I don't want to think today, Darrell." But, of course, I was thinking. Damned hermit!

"You see," he lectured, "the sequestered, highly local communities that once abounded in these hills, clustered about five miles apart, evaporated in the mid and late 20th Century after Scenic Byway Seven and other roads were paved, connecting the area with the world. A simple hike down a trail or fading road through the trees tells you the story: scattered and crumbled foundations, fallen chimneys, dry wells, overgrown farmsteads, forsaken lifetime efforts." He kicked aside some leaves, and there was a level chunk of cement—a visual aid!

"I have heard about the little villages..."

"On every side, just beyond the tree line, remnants of towns abandoned by even the ghosts, molder away under a snag of vines and rusty barbed wire. Take your pickup, someday, and drive back in—penetrating the now-reclaimed slopes dropping away from the paved highway of the ridge. It soon becomes an off-road ordeal of broken stone walls, flattened industrial sites, dead and empty barns and houses and schools and stores, sometimes just holes in the ground—all swathed in briars and skewered by grown-up hardwood trees. All very picturesque: so beautiful it would take embarrassing, unmanly poetry to describe it."

"Here now! There's nothing unmanly about poetry." I knew that Double-Dog was a literary man, a poet. We had clashed. And today he was being eloquent—no "hayseed" in his language, to speak of. He could turn that off and on at will. And he was always eloquent when he was gloomy.

"The highway was built as a lifeline, but it became a

hemorrhaging artery! Wars have left less devastation. The Wilderness is re-taking the territory. Naturally, it is gorgeous."

"Well, I like it here. It's quiet."

"The Buffalo National River thing blew up in our faces, too. Back in the early seventies your federal government came out and threw people off their land—veterans, some of them, who had fought for this country. They uprooted entrenched generations of people and tore out all signs of man and mathematics. Today you can go down there and rent a canoe and see it all the way it was before modern man lived here: trees, water, rocks, sky. Absolutely beautiful. But then you almost have to leave. That is the idea of Tourism. Come here, spend a little money, and then for God's sake and your own, please leave."

"The river is beautiful. I hear it's one of the purest in America." I couldn't quote any statistics. But I knew he was a man who liked to stay hydrated. Water. Water is good, right?

"National Forests and designated Wilderness Areas surround everything, and they are for 'visits' also! We are saving this place for whoever survives living in our snake pit cities. The young people all leave—have to. You can't make a living here. Look at what happens in town. You have a real estate/soda fountain/mortuary, or a feed store/tire shop/pizza parlor, or a TV repair/manicure/eyebrow waxing joint. Multi-tasking for survival! And shoulder-to-shoulder antique shops, flea markets, yard and garage sales, and perpetual going-out-of-business sales. Gas stations are as rare as doctors."

"Well, our needs are few..."

"Everything needed anywhere is needed here; it's just needed by older people! An audience here looks like a field of dandelions gone to seed. But you have to empty out many a square mile to come up with an audience, even a gray one. Hell, our chief import is Retirees."

"Thank you. Glad to help populate the hills."

"The only steady industry here is logging, the life's blood of the area. Murdering the trees keeps people alive here—and helps satisfy the appetites of cities full of selective idealists who say, 'Save the trees, but send the lumber, too.' The only growth industry is the nursing home, or worse, the hospice. If there is a viable year-round industry that rears its ugly head, somebody sends it to Mexico. Life here feeds on death, rot is beautiful, beautiful covers ugliness, blackberry patches mask rusting piles of garbage..."

"Darrell," I said, "I've got to get back to the house. Great little paradox, though."

"You wanna talk about a paradox? How about this: we live out here amid breath-taking, heart-stopping beauty, and half of these people have pacemakers or are carrying oxygen bottles! These are the vital people who are laboring away to keep alive the by-passed places, the skills, the crafts and arts we might have to return to if there is to be a future!"

"Bummer." Okay, so I was around high school kids too long. I should have gone with being speechless.

"When they're all driven out of the cities by mushroom clouds or worse, what we managed to save out here is all they will have. We are noble beings among Natural beings, nurturing the tiny, dim embers of this particular burnt-out section of civilization."

"Yup. Well, it's been good talkin' to yuh. I have to say, though, I never thought about it that way. I was all wrapped up in the trees, the sky, the fallen leaves, thinking good thoughts. I guess the new trees feed on these fallen leaves, though. It all fits together."

"You were thinking about Chinese food. I heard you say so."

"Yeah. Well, not any more."

"There's a good one in Branson, you know—and a nice new one in Harrison. Chinese buffet."

"Good. We'll look into it. Wifey and me."

I escaped through the woods. Double-Dog Darrell's Social Security check would hit the bank in a day or two, and then a nice crunchy prescription would make him sweet and docile again. I took some of what he said seriously, though. It is indeed miraculous that you can get acceptable moo goo guy pan in the Ozarks. The rest of it? Why tinker with bliss?

Canoe Fever

A sleek canoe, gliding on a placid stream amid reflections of a magic, natural tapestry of rock and tree and flower. A happy camper, for a change, returning to his primal roots, reading his history in the layers of stone in the faces of the cliffs at every bend of the river. Now and then a lagoon, deep and limpid, alive with merry fish. Primitive. Impressive.

And when we first saw the happy folks in canoes on the Buffalo National River, Wifey and I were impressed. Our new home in the mountains was a Mecca for people who wanted to put a canoe into a river and "float" past cliffs several stories high on waters among the clearest in America. They came for various reasons, and took away various rewards and lessons. They came by the hundreds, rented colorful canoes from outfitters who would "put them in" at one point on the 125 mile course, and "take them out" downstream a few miles. It was the local industry.

"I think we need a canoe," I told Wifey. "A canoe of our own. And a couple of colorful life preservers like they all wear: yellow or red—something vivid. And maybe we could get one of those little motors to drop over the side, just in case we needed it. Paddles , of course. We could have it any color you want. A fiber glass one, though—not an aluminum one. You can fix fiber glass if it gets punctured. And I think it should be a long canoe: one of the bigger ones. No sense getting by with a dinky one when we can be comfortable."

Wifey mumbled something or other. It doesn't matter what. Probably.

"Then maybe we could get a trailer to get it back and forth to the river. A trailer hitch shouldn't cost too much. Or I could get racks and carry it on top of the car. And I could rig up some mountings and have it on the side of the garage for storage. We could get one locally—new or used. But I think I'd like a new one. They manufacture them somewhere around here. I could look into it..."

"Please pass the salt," said Wifey.

"It could be blue, I guess. But I think we should get a good one. I've seen 'em at WalMart, but the ones made locally are classics. People from all over buy these canoes. And of course they could tell us about those numbers they have on them. We wouldn't have to fish. We could just float: go out and put in at Steele Creek and maybe get out at Kyle—or put in at Kyle and go down to Pruitt. Of course, we could go down river a ways. Might have to portage at the low-water bridge out by Hasty. I've seen them do that a few times. But we could do this. It would be a good way to see a lot of wonderful scenery we don't get to see up top."

"Need a refill?" said Wifey, wielding the Diet Coke two-liter.

"Thanks. Green. They make a lot of green canoes. We could stand it up in a rack beside the garage, or put a rack right on the side of the garage and store it horizontally. Or we could just leave it mounted on the trailer. We could get a cooler that floats, fill it with ice and cokes, and just chill—cover whole stretches of the river without a lot of work. And we wouldn't need to fish or camp—just get out and come home at night."

"Try some meat loaf," Wifey muttered.

"We could make meat loaf sandwiches, put it in the floatation cooler, have some Diet Coke along, and just lay back and let the river have us. We could bring a blanket along, all sucked down into a trash bag with the vacuum cleaner like that guy on TV. Wouldn't take up any room. And, if we wanted to, we could roll out on the river bank and flop down on the blanket and just relax."

"Eat your broccoli."

"Yeah. And maybe we could paint our own canoe: polka dot or paisley or peppermint striped. Hey, we could go with red, white, and blue: make a real patriotic statement. Go all the way to Tyler Bend..."

"Broccoli needs a little salt. But not a lot."

"Purple. Royal purple. We could come up with something really distinctive. And it's good exercise. We'd probably blow a few pounds in the process. Fiber glass. Little trailer, maybe. Or racks. Racks are good. You can do a lot with racks. I've seen lots of canoes go by on top of a car. Blue and green and yellow and...Well, maybe not purple. Purple would be too much."

"On the Fourth of July, we are going to rent a canoe and go with Betty and Jan on a little float trip. It is all set. We arranged it last week, and I told you all about it at the time."

"Betty and Jan?"

"I suppose you've never heard of Betty and Jan."

"Well..."

"We have canoes reserved. On July 5, after we've done this thing, we'll talk about canoes. Did you hear that and understand that?" Wifey was in the kitchen already, clattering dishes.

"Fourth of July, Betty and Jan, river trip, all reserved and ready to go. Gotcha."

"You never listen."

I could not believe I had been so persuasive! Here was Wifey, rolling over for that canoe without apparent resistance, and I had not even trotted out my good stuff. I had said nothing about safety, the "cool" factor, the "keeping up with the Joneses" bit, or "broadening our horizons in our Senior years." How fortunate can a man be? And we had said nothing about money. Maybe Wifey had a secret desire for a canoe, too. Anyway, I had won, and I was pleased.

I resolved to buy Wifey a nice massage, or maybe a whole

deluxe Hot Springs package. That night I dreamed of my canoe, painted like birch bark, slicing across the mirror image of one of the Buffalo's many cliffs, with me stroking away with my favorite paddle. There were drums, and Native American tenors heralded my approach with song; I couldn't quite get the words. But then I woke up, stared out the window into the night very dramatically, thought impossibly deep and enigmatic thoughts, and went back to bed. The canoe was red that time, but the chant was there, and the lovely cliffs, and the water. Later, my shot glass bladder got me up again, and when I went back to sleep, my canoe was bright yellow, and I was wearing buckskin. And the Indians were throbbing away: Choctaw and Kickapoo.

On July 4, at 9 a.m., Betty and Jan and their rented canoe (red), and Wifey and I and our rented canoe (brown), were "put in" at Steele Creek. Huge cliffs, clear waters below, blue sky above, cool breezes, everything we could have asked for. Plenty of water. No fear of having to portage (drag) that canoe over a hundred yards of rocks now and then, like some visitors. Still, it looked manageable: "floating," right? We were gonna float. This was ideal. We launched with a vengeance. Hell, I had read up on canoeing. We were good to go.

A few yards downstream, Betty and Jan beached their canoe in a snag of brush in the shallows on the right bank. Well, it was the left bank to them, for they were going backwards at the time. While we were laughing at them, we came to a sudden halt, and then sat teetering atop the only rock in the middle of the river. Our bow was out front, though; we just hadn't been aware of the rock. A perfectly simple error.

Surprisingly fast, then, I began to suspect that just being able to go left and right and forward, more or less intentionally, was not enough skill for this day's river. There had been some rain, and there was more water than usual. "Reading" the river was going to be important. I reached back to the deep recesses of my mind for some Mark Twain. But that was "a whole 'nother river." In Cliff's Notes, they don't get technical about these things anyway.

We avoided the next mid-stream rock, and it was a good thing, too, because we were moving now—rather rapidly. When we turned to avoid the rock, we spun around backwards. I dug hard on the right side, and we laid up quietly along the bank again. Betty and Jan flew by, airborne, I believe, and screaming. We found their paddles quite soon, linked up with the girls themselves, fished them out of the water, and had a few laughs. The river is full of little surprises: fast and slow.

We decided that it would be better if we stayed behind the girls and let them move out ahead a little. If they had problems, we could help. Wifey and I were a good canoe team in those first few stretches. Very few mistakes. Having a canoe of our own was going to be neat, most likely.

The Buffalo does not have a lot of what could be called "white water," but there are some spots, apparently, where you don't just "float." The river would actually be closed if things got really dangerous. We knew about those things. The river was "do-able."

We learned that getting a canoe down out of a tree can be challenging. Staying within gunshot of another canoe can also be a problem. Whenever we caught up to Betty and Jan, we felt truly fortunate. Once, as I watched Betty's face disappear beneath our prow, having caught up to them was the only thing that saved the moment. Oh, Betty popped up astern right away, and I was able to see that because Wifey and I were performing a maneuver river experts call a "three sixty" at the time, as we tumbled over a waterfall. Betty and Jan had just performed the "end-over-end" maneuver. It is amazing how far a pair of paddles can go in just the short time it takes to get a canoe off the bottom, get your party down out of the trees, and get going again. I decided, from experience, that paddles are like skis. You can tether them to you if you want, but they're going where they're going when you crash. We put our act back together, using sticks and poles and our hands, and we set off again down the river.

Betty and Jan were drowning again when we came upon them, having performed a "barrel roll," but their canoe was nearby—a little scratched up and dented, but on the water and upright. It had simply expelled them both and fled to safety. And they held their paddles close to their bodies. We did not laugh at them, because we had spent a few minutes dragging our vessel through two inches of water because of a wrong turn. I insist that it was a turn. (Wifey still maintains that we were simply cast out of the mainstream into a little tributary.)

When the four of us were all in one pool together, water moccasins (normally poisonous, dangerous, and ornery) ran for their lives; the birds were silent; fuzzy critters on both banks took cover; the sun itself went under a cloud. It was obvious that we did not belong on that river, and that the plot was now concerned with surviving the recreation and getting to hell out of there.

And that was where we parted company. Wifey and I shot out ahead, thinking that we could just stop along the way and wait for them to catch up if we saw a particularly rough spot. Behind us, somewhere, were the worst canoeists we had ever seen, and we were not totally responsible. We rounded a bend, and the river dropped out from under us—that quick. We flailed away at the air and the water with our silly paddles, but the cart-wheeling we effected was a very bad idea. I looked up, and Wifey was above me, and above her was the river. Slow motion. It was brutal.

We thought of lashing our canoes together, but thought better of it. We thought of huddling together to keep warm, because we were all shivering; but someone has to be warm to keep warm and none of us were warm at all. We were wet, and everything near us was wet. I was certainly happy that the whole thing was not my idea, but I kept my mouth shut.

"Are we having fun yet?" asked Wifey with her beatific smile.

"Not that I have noticed," I said.

"Don't you just wish this canoe belonged to you? We could paint it, patch up the holes, put it up on the side of the garage," she said. "Racks. Racks are good. And a trailer, of course. Fiber glass!"

I looked at what was left of our canoe. We could fix it, probably. The rocks and sand bars, and that one log, had taken their toll. When we ran over Betty and Jan, well, that was bad—but it was not like when we hit them broadside. But they were out of control—spinning round and round going down the bubbly part of the river. We, because of our skills, were going straight ahead at the time. It was certainly their fault.

There's a bag of trail mix down on the Buffalo somewhere, and a six pack of Diet Coke, and an ice chest that sinks. Sun glasses, too, and a blanket in a plastic bag with the air sucked out of it. And Betty and Jan lost a lot of sun block, some of those hair doodads, some nose plugs, a coupla hats, some sandwiches. Stuff like that. And they froze to death, almost, as did we. The river has cold springs feeding into it at every spot where people normally wipe out. It's all been calculated for the enjoyment of the tourist.

Oh, and when you have one foot in each of a pair of canoes, that doesn't work at all. You get wet, and it hurts. You end up giving the canoe people wet money. Of course, they're used to that and probably have a money dryer in the back room somewhere. And when you see them at the end of your river "float" trip, you want to hug them and hold them: hold someone, because you no longer have each other.

Wifey and I stayed together because we were tired of games and searching and loneliness. But we don't see Betty and Jan that much anymore. Never intentionally. We have what is called a "strained relationship" by river experts.

A Season of the Fingertips

Berry Picking Time, as devotees know very well, is a season of the fingertips. You feel a tingle all across the complicated patterns of your fingerprints, and something primal, deep inside you, starts pulling at you—luring you out of doors, sending you down old roads with your eyes peeled, looking for tell-tale red clues, arching branches (green and thorny), and privacy. You hunt for berries everywhere you go, and when you find them, you must have them. You are helpless, perhaps cursed.

In the summer of 2002, the raspberries were out there in the mountains around our hermitage in the Ozarks. Wifey and I had been watching the progress of those on the steep mountainside down in the village, and, of course, about the time one should begin picking, a swarm of locals descended upon the biggest patch and grabbed the berries by the bucket! It was fair. The berries there belonged to the villagers, I felt: right of proximity and all that. But I had found a patch of my own much earlier, and I was not talking to anybody about it. Those berries were mine. When everything was right, Wifey and I hit my secret patch and lugged away buckets and buckets.

But blackberry season was next. Just about the time the raspberries are ready to fall off the vines from over-ripeness, the blackberries are ready. For weeks I had watched my secret blackberry patch, and I knew that my timing was going to be perfect. The patch was The Mother Lode: the best blackberry patch I had ever seen. And it was accessible! It was laid out along an old timber road for about a half mile: just absolutely hung with berries, ripening in the sun afforded the patch by the road slashed through the tall trees. There were sparse spots, but there were also huge entanglements of intertwined, hostile, barbed and prickly blackberry brush so loaded with green berries that I was ecstatic. When they turned red, I was in heaven. I calculated the exact day that I should hit the patch and harvest the black gold!

Down at the county shed, as I now realize, hard and heartless men were watching my movements. I was probably seen skulking around the back roads and then frequenting the one where my blackberries were developing. They—the BIG THEY—observed me, watched me, and formulated a plan. When the time was right and I finally showed up with four large buckets all ready to reap the harvest, I found that the county road crews had come through with machines and digested my entire half-mile berry patch. There was not even a shadow of a sprig of stubble left of all those berries.

I stared in disbelief. I examined the bald ground where the patch had been. Gone. Utterly gone. I resolved to pout for the rest of the day. I vowed revenge. I began to plot and scheme. I sought out names and addresses. I searched on the Internet for spells and charms and curses to hurl at my enemies. I prayed. But the berries were gone. Just to make sure, I went down to the county compound and crept up close to the chain-link fence and eyeballed the equipment parked there. Sure enough: a tractor and a heavy-duty bush hog were stained with blackberry juice! Indelible proof. Evil doers for sure.

Non-berry-picking friends told me to grow up, accept the blow, get on with life. Somehow, I was to understand that other people had other scenarios, and that there was nothing personal about the atrocity they had committed. Having someone hit would be an overreaction. The road workers were just doing their job. Blackberry brush is a nuisance. It had to go. I was being paranoid. There would be other berries in other places.

Cold comfort. Those were my berries, and they were taken from me. In the Bible Belt, some would say that they were God's berries, and that He chose to have them ground up into useless mulch this year. My error was in thinking that they were

MY berries in the first place. "The Lord giveth and the Lord taketh away." And all of that said to me that God was punishing me, probably for not going to church and catching Hell every Sunday.

"Jesus, they wiped out the whole damned patch!" I moaned. A religious thought.

Wifey put the word on the street: We need a new berry patch and we need it now. But the county street sweepers came along and ruined that. (That's probably a metaphor.) I searched other little side roads and paths, old logging roads and abandoned fence lines and driveways; we gave broad hints out to our friends; as a last resort, we searched our own property. And all of the blackberry patches that we found were barren, diseased, sickly, or sterile. The county boys had wiped out the only viable patch around. I sank into a deep depression.

Berries have appeal because they are free, because it takes effort to get them, because they are beautiful, and because they are good for you. Ecologically, they are Politically Correct. They should not go to waste, and if they are not picked, they will most assuredly fall to the ground, useless. Birds harvest only a few of them: there are only a few birds. Usually, it takes a lot of sugar to make jellies and jams from berries. It is not an economic thing we are talking about here. Like game, it costs too much per pound ever to be practical. But if you go out there, get scratched up and eaten alive by bugs, and come away with a bucket of berries, that is Victory, and it is obeying God! I insist. And men who get in the way of berry pickers will probably rot in Hell.

In time, I was informed that, "It's just not a good year for blackberries. Best wait for the elderberries."

Elderberries? There are elderberries? How does that work? I had seen them, of course, but they seemed so small, so work intensive. But there are oceans of them when things are right. I found out about them: the white blossoms, the huge heads with hundreds of tiny berries, and the acknowledged best technique of gathering them and extracting the blessed juices. I spotted piles and piles of them, and I resolved to wait them out.

But what about the county boys? Would they not try to destroy my elderberries, too? I was certain by then that, deep in the bowels of the county courthouse, there was an Office of Berry Eradication. I would have to have a stratagem: I would have to feign indifference, throw attention away from the elderberries, perhaps even take a trip off mountain and out of county. I knew if my interest in the elderberries became common county knowledge, the machines would roll, and MY elderberries would be mulched, in an act of bitter spite, by heartless, demonic county drones.   N   o way I could arm myself and guard all the berry places, either; however, very soon, started fantasizing about popping up out of my elderberry patch and machine-gunning the blade of the bulldozer as it approached—about painting myself up with camouflage make-up and lurking in the bushes, then leaping on some county scum-bag and slicing his throat with my black bayonet—about booby-trapping my elderberries and blowing the county wrecking crew to kingdom come. Petty, shameful, melodramatic, selfish embarrassing thoughts.

I began having intellectual conversations about it with my wife, too.

"Give it a rest," my wife said. "It's just berries. You can get jams and jellies at WalMart for a little of nothing."

"But..."

"Just let it drop. It's not worth all this passion."

"But..."

"I don't want to hear any more about berries."

"But..."

"Next year."

"Yes, Dear."

I lost the argument. But I won the war. In my ramblings, I found a magnificent patch of elderberries, just loaded, just boiling out of the road ditch, coming after the county road like they wanted to shut down traffic. It was perfect, and I visited it regularly, even getting out of the car and fondling the huge blossom heads. I even made notes on a large calendar I had there in the front seat. Once, I even got out with a berry bucket and poked through the patch. I looked at my watch. I paced up and down. I scanned the area with binoculars. If the county boys were watching me (and I could feel their evil eyes on me out there, make no mistake), they could get no other impression than this was MY berry patch, and that I was going to reap the harvest.

The berries went through the green nodule phase, into the red phase, then to a darkish red. They would be black when ripe. I toyed with them—the rotters from the Berry Eradication Department—as they skulked in the tall weeds they left standing near the patch so that they would have cover for their surveillance. They were out there, like things in a Stephen King cornfield, waiting. There were signs. I know these things. I insist.

But while they were timing their attack, I was doing a little timing myself.

The county boys ripped through the patch during the darkish red phase. This time, I watched them. They hit it first with a tractor with a sickle bar, then a bush hog that splattered everything to smithereens and flung it off into the woods. Utter carnage. Once, I thought I saw one of them look around at the trees, probably wondering if I was watching, heartbroken, out there in the green gloom. I was out there, all right, but I was smiling.

I took ten buckets of elderberries out of my secret patch— the patch I never let them see. It was on our own land—just over the cliff. Nothing the county owns will go there. I had to rope up and rappel down to them, but they were mine. Buckets and buckets: deep black and juicy—practically forbidden fruit in our county!

I whipped up a beautiful sign: ELDERBERRIES FOR

SALE—BUCKETS AND BUCKETS! And I tacked it up in the county courthouse, with my name, address, and phone number. Of course, whenever someone called about the berries, we told them we were sold out! I just wanted the county boys to know that I had beaten them down like dogs.

Berry-Picking is serious stuff.

The Gathering

I don't know why you think you can sit there and sneer at me and make pathetic jokes. I know what I'm talkin' about. And, I tell you, the so-called 'Friends of the Library' are up to no good." Wifey and I were being lectured again by the neighbor lady.

We had asked about cultural matters downhill in the town. All through the hills we had seen signs of the struggle: a wilderness of overgrown, crumbling foundations where industries, businesses, homes, and whole communities had once thrived. The county was apparently a place that used to be. And now it seemed to be occupied by people who used to be: people like us. It was a retired county, and we were retired people. But Wifey and I reasoned that there must be a local effort to hang on to cultural things. We were not ready for culture to be some remote thing in the past or at the distant ends of the narrow strip of tar that ran through the heart of the place. There must be others like us—some aged version of Sinclair Lewis' Carol Kennicott, maybe. (Old English teachers do struggle so.) Still, we should have known better than to ask the neighbor lady about such matters.

"I've heard about a library group," said Wifey. "What do they do?"

"Those are the people who got those Harry Potter books back on the shelves, you know," our friend said smugly. "They want that filth available to our children."

Well, I could not stay quiet about that. "Probably not a book burner in the bunch."

"They *should* have a fire and burn all of those sorcery books. They're about a school for sorcerers, you know."

"If you ban Harry Potter, the children will see what you have done and be frightened and ashamed."

"Those books teach witchcraft!" she almost shrieked.

"By banning those books, adults teach children that *they* believe in witchcraft, whether the kids do or not. I don't believe in witches, do you?"

"Don't you know Double-Dog Darrell? He's a warlock, you know." Yeah, her eyes were as big as basketballs again. We had hit a nerve.

"Oh, My God. I knew he was eccentric, but I thought he was mortal. I have pictures of him. He shows up on film. I have seen his shadow and his reflection. I did not realize he was supernatural. And I did not know he was with the fiendish library people."

"None of them are up to any good. The whole tribe of them are all in league with the devil."

And that is when I sneered and scoffed and made bad jokes. The neighbor lady was not amused. She was a little miffed, and she began to hiss and roll her eyes, checking for eavesdroppers, or THEM!

"On Friday nights, there are strange doin's down at that library," she whispered. "There is a 'gathering.' Lights go out. Things are being done there."

"It's probably a book study group," offered Wifey. "Sometimes, in the paper..."

"In the dark?" charged the neighbor lady. "They read in the dark?"

"Maybe they have discussions, book reviews—meetings."

"It's called a 'gathering,'" the neighbor lady corrected, "and it's done in the dark. It's not normal."

"Well, really, what in Heaven's name could happen in the county library in a dinky little town—with such straight, humble, God-fearing people?"

"Where do you think these things happen? You lived in the city too long. You think everything bad happens in the city. Wake up and smell the boondock brimstone! And don't let some people hear you use the words 'in Heaven's name' and 'God-fearin'' in the same sentence where you're talkin' about the library bunch!"

"This is fascinating," I said (baiting her). "All in the dark, you say. This is absolutely juicy."

"They're up to something. I've heard things. That one librarian—the good looking young lady? You can tell she's not an innocent. I hear she has a tattoo. And there's a man that sits around in there a lot, hunkered over a computer, sometimes with no socks on, and he looks at people over the top of his glasses. And Double-Dog Darrell was seen there."

"Sounds scandalous," I offered. I tried to recall a good looking young lady, and I decided that she was talking about a good looking lady in her early fifties. But in this county, that's arguably young. All young people are suspected of evil intentions or actions, just as people over thirty are beyond trust to the young. A good-looking lady would explain Double-Dog Darrell's involvement. The computer with no socks on was more challenging.

"Hard tellin' what they do with the money they get for fines. And they get state money, too, and they have book sales at the flea markets, and pie suppers, and they raise funds by having a dinner every year out at the cave house."

"That anywhere near The Bottomless Pit?"

"Go ahead and mock me. But mark my words: that library mob is evil."

"My dear, we must get ourselves down to the library," I said to Wifey. "It sounds like a diabolical conspiracy is afoot—back in the stacks, perhaps, or in the mysterious back rooms where the public is not supposed to go. No telling what they're doing down there on that thick carpet in the children's area (with the tiny furniture), or around corners and out of sight."

"Yeah, right."

"I know what I know," said the neighbor lady. "You may have to learn the hard way. Remember this conversation."

At that point, we deliberately diverted the course of

our deliberations—to preserve the general harmony of The Ridge. Ours was a small neighborhood, and we did not need to pollute the atmosphere with any refusal to play the game. The Devil, witches and warlocks, ghosts and goblins, evil spirits and the like were all literary characters to us: entertaining and stimulating. If there were any in the library, we were sure they were between the covers of books, and quite manageable. To the neighbor lady, however, these things were real, and those who did not believe in them did not believe in God, either, and she had no time for them. Touchy situation for us. Unstable ground. We ducked and ran.

But we had to hook up with the library bunch, of course. The neighbor lady had devils all over her house and yard, and we could not seem to help her. But downhill in the town, the "library mob" was throbbing away, from all reports, and we decided that we must penetrate the inner circles as soon as possible and discover their secrets. I had fun imagining a coven of baleful, bookish characters, all gathered in a tight circle in the hushed calm of the county library, hatching devilish schemes and contracting for souls, concocting potions and curses and spells, probably naked and deformed—perhaps hoofed! I dreamed up mysterious bookcases behind which the Gates of Hell yawned and fumed, and the horned Demons of Literacy swarmed about springing the trap on unsuspecting patrons. The more I thought about it, the more twisted it became. It was time to make the Friday night scene, for starters.

As we drove past the library on Wednesday afternoon, I noticed that there was a peculiar aura about the place. We had been there many times in the past, but all of that was before we knew that the Library Mob was up to no good. Now there was a menacing black cloud hanging over the building. The neat little rock garden out front was now a cemetery in shallow disguise; the drive-thru portico took on the appearance of a giant mandible, waiting; the dark windows became eyes; the board-and-batten walls showed an apparent plague of knot holes—warts and carbuncles and pustules running dark ooze. I could see it all. I worked and developed the fantasy.

By Thursday, I was giggling over images of The Library Mob administrating the neighbor lady's Bottomless Pit (one of her favorite places in the county), entertaining themselves with pornography, wheeling soulless bodies around on library carts, reading demonic texts while squatting around a pentagram on the floor of the children's reading area, and plotting the accumulation of the last hold-out souls in the county! I merrily thumbed through an imagined Devil's Card Catalogue, browsed the closed stacks where the satanic volumes were hidden, and consorted with book worms amid spider webs and ancient, sulfuric dust. We saw suspicious vehicles parked at the library on our way back from the Senior Citizens' Center: Fords and Dodges and even a PT Cruiser. I noted the good looking woman's little car: catlike and poised to spring! Red, too. There were probably brooms in that library, too.

Yeah. Time to pay this place a little Friday night visit. Time to crash the party.

It was a dark and stormy night. We had invited our neighbor to join us in our invasion of the inner sanctum of the library, but she preferred to stay home on such nights. The bears and pumas in her yard, the witches and warlocks at the library, and, of course, lightning and thunder—all discouraged her. We put our vehicle into a dive and descended to the village, losing a little rubber on the sharp curves, and arrived quickly, braking and yanking to the left at the library's driveway. The headlights lit up a license plate I may never forget: 666 IHS. We arrived howling with laughter.   The Library Mob was there ahead of us. Well, most of them were. Someone was popping some popcorn in the microwave in the mysterious backroom (which had a kitchenette as its most sinister feature). The core event of The Gathering had not begun. The warlocks were opening some two-liter coke bottles, and a couple of the hellish handmaidens were setting out some Styrofoam bowls and some salt. Books were everywhere, and those present could not keep their hands off them. Their leader rose and approached the VCR with a rectangular black box. She smiled just briefly, a little enigmatic, impish grin, quick and deadly. All present seemed to know us and expect us. And we fell in with them.

In mere minutes we were sitting in the dark with The Library Mob, and we were watching *Casablanca*. We had crossed over. We were now among the unclean.

A Man and His Dog House

My dog house project was a triumph and a wonder: good strong 2 x 4 frame, cypress siding, composition shingles—even some thick "R-Board" insulation! Custom-sized door, curtained by Wifey. I was proud, and Wifey was pleased. (I still think that today.) Ginger did not like it or accept it, but Ginger snapped her chain one day and stepped out onto Highway 7 at the wrong time about a week after I drove that last nail, and, alas, my dog house was my dog house indeed.

And it sat there for a while, reminding us of our loss. I had built a tool box once in shop class in junior high, but Ginger's place was my first large scale structure. I painted it the color of our house: Sahara Dune, or some such hue; I caulked it—sealed it tight—weather-proofed it; I committed a fine blanket to its plywood floor. Then Ginger hated it, seemed to fear it, barked at it. I was glad she was a female, because I could imagine leg-lifting and spritzing, et cetera. Unoccupied, then, ever, Ginger's house sat there and made us think of our dog: our last dog, our final dog, the one whose loss put us past mere sadness and well into despair.

"The dog house has to go," said Wifey, finally; and I knew she was right.

"But…" I argued valiantly.

"Burn it; tear it apart; sell it. But get rid of it."

I would have sat staring at the flames to the last pathetic ember, written a sad dozen or so couplets, and sobbed my romantic heart out—if I had tried to burn the thing. Every splinter of it would have reminded me of Ginger— if I had torn it down. But sell it? I had not thought of that. How would one sell a dog house? Especially around here?

Wifey and I had moved from the city into the Ozark Mountains two or three years earlier. Our city dog, a big German Shepherd, had been a heartbreak. We had been forced to have him "put down" because of incurable miseries; and when that happened, that was about it for the city, and dogs. We retired, found a mountaintop, and settled in. Then we saw Ginger in a WalMart parking lot. One last dog.

"Take out an ad in the local weekly; put up a sign at the grocery store; get a realtor on it. Just get rid of it." Wifey was adamant.

"But…"

I wanted to tell her that I had built that house with my bare hands, that it was square and plumb and sturdy and tight, that it was a noble and magnificent creation rendered with love and respect and even art! But she was right. It had to go. But how?

"Just put it out along the highway with a sign on it," said the neighbor lady. "That's how it's done around here. Someone will stop if they are interested." Her advice concerning local mores had always seemed sound. She had studied things—as an outsider, from Iowa.

Made sense to me. I sat up half the night arriving at what I thought was a fair price, and the morning after that vigil I hooked onto the dog house with a dolly and wheeled it out to the end of the driveway, close to Scenic Highway 7; and I put up a well-lettered sign: For Sale, Dog House, $50.

The sign rotted: faded and dried up in the sun and then drooped and sagged and slid down into a puddle of muck beside the dog house. That was summer. I made a new sign: Dog House For Sale, $40. That one blew away with the autumn leaves. My next sign, in late October, said, "Haunted Dog House, $25." Then I tried, "Turkey House, $20." Then, "Dog House. Make Offer."

"You have to be ready to deal," said the neighbor lady. "These people like to haggle and finagle and wangle. They respect shrewdness and cunning. You have to be ready to stand your ground." And I believed that.

"I just want to get rid of it before I have to live in it," I said to her, smiling toothily at Wifey.

"Don't let them know that," the neighbor told me, almost hissing. (It's hard to hiss when there are no esses.)

So, I prepared for that encounter. I was going to be fair, but firm. If someone wanted to talk about that dog house, I was going to be a savvy dealer, a clever opponent. I was going to get respect, but I was going to sell that dog house, too, and gain a local reputation as someone who had moved out from the city but had made the grade. I would not be a pushover, a sap, a sucker. I was an educated man, after all, and a builder! I had fended for myself in the city. I had driven daily in the toughest traffic in the country. I had gone toe-to-toe with plumbers and house inspectors and realtors. I had even been through a divorce. I could handle this.

Just before Christmas, an old red pick-up pulled into the driveway, and a little old man, bent and trembling, slowly stepped down onto the crushed limestone surface, right next to the dog house. He was a local, I noticed, probably on his way to the village for some hard tack and beans and flour. Or pizza. I stayed cleverly hidden for a minute or two, and then, when it was time to "set the hook," I made my move.

"Howdy," I said, chewing on a piece of straw I had cleaned up earlier for the scene. I was wearing my bib overalls, too. It was perfect.

"They'll dance around," I could hear the neighbor lady saying. "They'll pretend to be only casually interested. They'll try to make you think they're doing you a favor to take it off your hands. Stand firm. They'll fake walking away. Call their bluff. It's a game, and they love to play it."

I was ready for him. I was going to pluck this pigeon like a...Never mind.

"How much you want fer this dog house?" said the old man.

"Clever," I thought. "Wiley. He thinks he has me off

balance. I can handle this." I looked him straight in the eye.
Well, I bent down a little, and I looked him straight in the eye.
"How much am I offered?" I thought he might say something
ridiculous, like $10, or $7.50. I thought he was going to scorn my
work, criticize the paint color, or pretend to be poor. I thought
he was going to say $15, and pull out some pathetic old leather
purse and unsnap it with trembling hands, wheezing. I thought
we were going to bat dollar amounts back and forth and arrive
at something like $12.87. I thought he might trot out a cute
granddaughter with a puppy that looked like Ginger. But these
things are never simple. Never.

"Young fella," he said instead, "I couldn't be the sort of a
man that would stop along a road, go on another man's land, and
tell him what his property was worth."

We were definitely talking about *me* now. He was sincerely
hoping that I was not so lowly and vile as to presume that
he was the sort who would sink to such base behavior that
he would have the effrontery to violate the sanctity of the
hallowed ground that I had wrenched from the clutches of The
World by the sweat of my brow—as he had doubtlessly done
himself (a brother man)—on another mountain, beside another
road—at another time—a tougher time—with perhaps greater
effort. We were both nobler men than that! Unless I had no
nobility in me!

Well, it was over. I was beaten. Unaccountably, I felt
embarrassed at having pre-judged the old man as an opportunist.
Which, of course, he was. But I was the bad guy suddenly. Or
maybe all along. I don't know. I stood there, twisting in the
wind: totally nonplussed. My mouth went dry. I quickly scrolled
through Panic, Disgust, Total Confusion, Amusement, Deep
Respect, Denial, Self-Loathing, Guilt, Rationalization, and
Despair. Finally, I suggested $5, and he had that amount in his
hand: that exact amount. He held it out to me and winked.

I took my pittance and went into the house—after loading
the dog house into the venerable old gentleman's truck. I tried

for a week to think of what I could have said to him. Then I tried for another week. But he had called me "Young Fella," right out there in my driveway. And he had presented me with layers of consideration that still wake me in the night. Go figure.

I told Wifey that I got $20.

The Day I Almost Lost the Feed Store

I f you work around chain saws long enough, you'll come up short." That's the way Lefty Sawyer put it. "Just ask Old Stumpy Walker—or Wheels Vandergrift."

I believed him right away. I was down at the feed store, trying to get my manhood back, and Lefty Sawyer was helping me.

Manhood, and especially what is considered manhood in a certain locale, is very important. Vision quests, circumcisions, trials by fire, drinking vile substances and eating horrible concoctions, killing things, capturing and trapping and gathering myriad objects, enduring tortures, yada yada yada. There's a lot of that on record. Whatever works, right?

With most modern males, it has been simpler; and yet, there is always some key factor that means Manhood: getting your own car, owning a Harley, losing your virginity, shooting a deer, in some areas—with a bow and arrow, for God's sake! In some ghettos, it's all about committing your first crime—even murder! Making your bones!

I do not remember what it was in Minnesota, but I think it had to do with facing 52 below zero. You didn't feel or look like a man out there in that cold (with your nose running), but there was a ruggedness to it. As with heroism, there's probably a "choice" factor involved. We had little choice about the cold.

I thought I got there, though: Manhood! I even became a father! And I was, for many years, a teacher/mentor/role model, and all that—for many, many years—in a big city, in a multi-ethnic high school. That qualified me for combat pay, and I got it. Then I retired, dropped out, and went away. That's where

this was: away. And around here, Manhood is all tied into chain
saws.

In the hardwood forests of America, there exists a breed
of men who live and die by the chain saw. Many of them cut
their teeth on one in childhood. Where we were living, and
all through the woods around us, when someone trusted you
enough to hand you a chain saw, you had arrived, and you could
walk like a man into the feed store.

Nobody handed me mine, and that's different. I brought it
out from the city: a sissy chain saw with a bar about a foot long:
embarrassing, and, well, short. It was green, too. I kept it out
of sight as long as I could. I hadn't earned a chain saw, and this
pathetic thing kept reminding me.

It would start, and I could cut through small limbs, and I
was very careful. I was terrified of the thing! (I had seen the
movies, too, where a fiend chases women through the woods,
wielding a chain saw.) It seemed to me that the business end
of the saw was just waiting for me to make a mistake: then it
would grab my hand and shred it, or it would tear a slash across
my poor thigh—out in the woods where I would be sure to
bleed to death. Or it would not start at all, throwing me into
the puzzle of its motor and its peculiar mixture of oils and gas. I
stayed away from the chain saw as much as possible.   But on
the mountain, you had to tangle with one sooner or later—and
then often! Like the cold of Minnesota, it was out there, and I
had to face it, and I did. I handled it like I would handle a live
skunk, or a dirty diaper: at arm's length, my nose up high and
out of danger. The jobs were large, and the tool was small and
overworked. Soon, my poor little green chain saw would not cut
hot butter. Then it would not start well, and then it would not
start at all. It was time to face the guys down at the feed store,
where chain saws are bought, sold, sharpened, and maintained.

I must explain that, if it were entirely up to me, I would

never have gone to the feed store with my chain saw at all—ever. Wifey made me go. At the feed store, I had observed, their chain saws were bigger than mine, and they had names like Stihl, and Black and Decker, and McCulloch. And they weren't green. Mine was a little French rig, and could just as well have been pink. They had saws that could cut down big oak trees in nothing flat. I had gnawed away at a little sumac bush for twenty minutes just before the impotent thing rolled over and died on me. Getting out of the woods, I stumbled and fell and broke said bush accidentally, the only progress of the day.

But I reported. I went down to the feed store and turned myself in, just to assuage Wifey. "Hi, there," I said, "I am a wimp with utterly no manhood. This tiny chain saw hasn't worked since my castration last week. My wife feels that you men will take pity on me and fix this thing so that I will be able to prune the roses..." Well, not really. But that's the way it felt when I brought the dainty toy in.

"What is that, a Norelco?" asked the nice man as I entered.

"Something like that. Water-Pic. Oster. I don't know."

"Son, y'awl need more chain saw than that around here." And I think the guy exchanged a knowing glance or two with another customer, a man wearing a John Deere cap and a pair of camouflage cover-alls.

"I know that, sir, but this is all I have right now."

"Sir? You talkin' about my ol' Daddy! He was Sir. I'm Just Ben."

"Okay, Ben, this thing is all the chain saw I have. Will you take a look at it?"

"Be better off with a good jackknife," he muttered as he took the green trinket and stepped into the back room.

I looked around the feed store. Multi-tasking was evident everywhere: the smells of denim and leather and rubber, grain and various oils, bolts and nails and wire! It was a farm supply store, a hardware store, a nursery, a bootery, an automotive shop: a sensual feast of tires, bib overalls, seed corn, boots, camouflaged hats and shirts, shovels and forks and pickaxes, stacks of mineral and salt blocks, veterinary supplies and medicines, insecticides side-by-side with fungicides and herbicides, and manly gloves and post-hole diggers! And barbed wire! Out back somewhere, I heard the snarl of a big chain saw. This was man country. They had a coke machine, too.

I felt like a piece of lace—like a tiny pearl-headed pin tossed into a box of sixteen penny nails—like a sissy in the Marines. I had the most pitiful chain saw in the hills, and I had to surrender it helplessly to men who maintained adult chain saws! Whatever was wrong with the beast, it would be my fault.

"Poor little thing's dead," the man reported, holding my little green machine out to me with two fingers. "Nothing we can do with it."

"Gone, huh?"

"Burnt up. Somebody must have been runnin' it without chain oil. Best get a new one." He eyed me grimly.

"Chain oil?"

Well, he rolled his eyes, and he knew the whole story immediately—and so did I. I was new in Chain Saw Land. How could I know about the chain oil? I had fused the blessed innards of the little green beast, and I was now pond scum, simply beyond redemption. Even the little chain saws were sacred to this man, and I was worse than a child molester for what I had done. It was all there in his eyes.

"How much is a new one?" I asked innocently.

"We don't have anything like this around here, Son, but if you decide to get into a real chain saw, we can talk a deal. You can put this one on a charm bracelet. But if I sell you a real one, you have to promise to take care of it." Son. I was sixty, and this guy was younger than I, and he was calling me Son. I felt like one of those pedophile priests. I had sinned grievously.

I made no promises. I mumbled something, ducked low, and wandered off among the merchandise in the store, getting a quick look at some of the rugged, durable-looking products in the chain saw area. Other customers came in wearing clothes they had purchased there, and I was discussed in hushed tones.

They were embarrassed for me and lowered their eyes rather than look straight at me. They shook their heads. I sidled toward the door and eventually and slipped outside and fled. It would be difficult to return, ever.

That very Christmas, however, there was a bright new chain saw under the tree, just for me. It was a McCulloch, and it had Manhood written all over it. Oh, there were bigger ones around, but I was not a timber man. I was never going to sling one of those things and climb up and top a tree, and I was never going to cut through the trunk of a huge oak and fell it, just so, and holler, "Timber!" (I've learned that that's a movie word anyway.) My needs were simpler. But I had instructions now on which substance to put where to make the saw work properly and safely. I read the whole manual. I had not regained my full manhood, but my self-respect was definitely making a comeback. Merry Christmas!

I went into the woods and absolutely laid waste to the stubborn saplings that had earlier frustrated me. I aired the place out good, making room for growth of the big trees. I took down the "junk" trees and left the hardwoods. We had white oak, red oak, walnut, hickory, cherry, and maple, along with some dogwood and redbud. The saw snarled and growled, and I cut a swath. I came out of the woods sweaty and arm weary, absolutely reeking: pretty close to manly. But my chain was dull now, and it needed to be sharpened.

The feed store guy was more receptive this time. I had obviously been working in the woods with my chain saw, and it was one that had some dignity. I was even wearing my bib overalls that day. He sent my chain into the back room for sharpening. It was going to cost three bucks. He said that most guys sharpened their own chains, but that he understood. He had sold Wifey the chain saw she gave me for Christmas. His personal chain saw was still bigger than mine, but mine was a tough little rascal, good for the small jobs. We even chuckled together a little, and he showed me the bigger rigs. I wisely tapped into his expertise: got him into lecture mode. He was pleased. The whole thing fired my imagination, and I thought about bringing down a really big tree someday. The man even patted my back, rather heartily. A brother Man!

Back in the garage, I put the chain back on the saw, and I hummed a little as I worked. A few months before, I would not have attempted any of the tasks I now considered routine. I could now use any number of tools, perform many difficult and dangerous tasks, and handle a chain saw. I had worked in brick and block and stone, in planks and plywood and sheetrock, in landscape timbers and cedar posts! I could remember when putting a chain on a saw would have been unthinkable to me: a complicated mechanical challenge. Now I would do anything! I was "cutting it." I tinkered and I hummed. Bass, of course.

A few minutes later, things started going sour. I took the chain saw out front to bob off a 4 X 4 that was protruding from the ground, part of a decorative fence I had removed. Piece of cake. No problemo. But the saw would not cut. It smoked and snarled, it raced and slowed down to nothing, I pushed and yanked, and I called that infernal instrument lusty names! The 4 X 4 barely got nicked.

"Those fools," I said to Wifey. "They can't sharpen the damned chains they sell you! Here they are, all wrapped up in that masculine crap, and they can't even sharpen the chain!" I was ticked.

"Take it back to them," she said. "Make them do it right."

"Damned straight," I said.

But that's not the kind of guy I am. I was not going to rush down the mountain with fire in my eyes and go after the men at the feed store and call them incompetent right to their faces. I was going to gripe about it for a few days, and then skulk back into their realm and suggest that they take a look at it. Wifey knew that. I was not into confrontations.

When I got out of bed the next morning, the house was quiet. Wifey was up and gone. And the chain saw was gone, too— all of it, not just the chain. It was one of those gut-wrenching epiphanies. I saw it all immediately. The whole nightmare came together in my mind, and I knew I was doomed. She was down there at the feed store giving those men a piece of her mind. I couldn't find one of her dresses or I would have put it on!

"I took your chain saw in," she told me later. "The man said that it would work just fine if you put the chain on right. You had it inside out and backwards—probably upside down, too. The man had such tears in his eyes that he could hardly work, but he put the chain on right."

Well, I was toast: milk toast—wet and limp and disgusting.

That is how I almost lost the feed store. I couldn't go back there for a long time. Wifey said that they all had a big laugh about it whenever she went there for seeds, feeds, or fertilizers. They couldn't even look at a chain saw without thinking of me. But down there in the village, at the feed store, among the chain saws—that's where Manhood was. And, until Lefty took me, I could not go there.

Holding up the stump of his right arm, Lefty said, "You've got to go on. The chain saw is gonna win one now and then—buck you off! But you gotta get back on him and keep goin'."

I told him of my embarrassment, and he said, "Where's my right hand? Now, that was embarrassing! Everybody here has put the chain on backwards. But Stumpy Walker? The saw got his foot. And Old Wheels Vandergrift? He screwed up twice! Don't let a simple mistake wreck you. You've got all your arms and legs!"

I could go to the feed store now, if I wanted to, but I wouldn't exactly spray testosterone around the place. I would maintain a low profile—sort of wall-up and stay quiet—and I would treat chain saws with reverence and respect. That is, if I were to go there sometime. And maybe get into some camouflage.

Below the Radar

The View was what we had bought. No gardener would have bought our place. He would have had to rope up to weed the pea patch: rappel down to it from the back deck. Mowing our "lawn" was an acrobatic act—an extreme sport. The house was an architectural abortion. It looked like something in the back row in the trailer park. Even the colors of the house and the little barn out back were a pain: black and blue, in fact, and a swatch or two of scab red. No, it was The View that we bought.

And The View could be different each morning, each hour, sometimes each minute. Sometimes it filled up with clouds and resembled a huge bowl of whipped cream; sometimes it looked like a lake of milk; sometimes it was clear and pristine and therefore full of details—clear, yet full of details. A small irony there. Each morning I fired up a Diet Coke and reported to the big window on the top floor of the alleged house, and I drifted off into whatever The View had to offer. That ritual became part of life.

But one morning a few weeks after our arrival on the mountain, I stepped to that window and was immediately blasted backwards. Coming straight at our windows from a point below the level of our little reservation was a huge aircraft: roaring uphill, right at my nose—mountain above it, valley below it, sky above everything! Then its white belly zoomed just above the downhill black walnut tree, then the shadow slid over the house, and it was gone. I screamed for my wife, but the noise of the plane drowned out the effort. Immediately another plane pulled the same maneuver, and then another. It was shattering.

"My God!" I screamed. "What the hell is THAT all about?"

Wifey knew exactly what to do. She had the neighbor lady on speed dial, and she made contact before the windows quit vibrating.

"It's military," the neighbor lady told us. "Those are what they call C-130s. Didn't have them in WWII. They're out here from Little Rock practicing flying below the radar."

"They fly too low," Wifey told her. "Below the radar is okay, but below our lower deck? Below our yard?"

"Kinda gets your attention, don't it?"

By then I was on the other phone. "Do they do this a lot?" I asked.

"Yeah. All the time. Not every day or anything, but a lot."

"The young captain—the guy with the mustache and the dark glasses—he was sneering," Wifey said.

"I think he is too young," I added, picking up the little joke. "The guy in the other seat had acne problems. It's kids they've got flying those things. My God!"

"Well, don't yell at me about it," the neighbor lady grumbled. "It's one of the many things I do not personally control." I could not imagine. "Besides, they're our boys."

Well, we couldn't really see the crew that well, of course. It was all too fast. But they were low, and I was reminded of the attack on Pearl Harbor where someone reported looking out their window and into the cockpit of a Japanese plane—seeing the pilot's face and his streaming scarf—and a little smile.

I wanted to write to the base in Little Rock and mention some of the details of the planes: rivets, oil streaks, minor tool scratches, etc., but I refrained. "Dear General," I wanted to write, "The young fella who flew through my living room this morning flies too low. We lost dishes. Any way I can persuade you to have him fly elsewhere? Or higher?"

"You have a neighbor who will cut loose any minute. Just cock an ear and listen," the neighbor lady said. I could imagine her eyes getting bigger. This was juicy for her.

"What do you mean?" said Wifey.

"Just open your door and listen."

And so we did. It was not long before we heard semi-automatic rifle fire in the direction of one of our close neighbors. (Well, he lives within a half-mile of us, really, and out on the mountain that's close.) Over twenty shots, about as fast as he could pull the trigger. An AR-15, most likely. Then about six louder shots, I thought from a big pistol, like a 44 magnum. Then eighteen shots from a .22 rifle—something I knew about personally. Then it was over. All of the shooting happened in the time it takes to tell it. Bangedy bang.

"Okay, what was that for?" I asked the lady on the phone.

"Every time we get buzzed, he goes outside and empties two or three guns."

"Not at the planes!"

"No, just into the woods. Sometimes he re-loads and does it again. He was in Viet Nam."

"But the VC didn't have planes like that."

"It's just a sound from those days, and it drives him up the wall. A chopper is worse. He goes out back, and he shoots. Some do dope, some drink. Harold shoots."

"Well, does he think he's being attacked, or what?"

"Don't ask me. And, for God's sake, don't ask him! He just shoots. Then it's over. He'll be quiet now, until next time."

Now I really wanted to write to the base in Little Rock, tell them the whole story, and get them to quit violating our neighborhood air space. Or I wanted to notify the sheriff that some nut was shooting up the woods. Or something. But I also wanted to mind my own business, get along with the people I had to live with, and try to understand this new environment. I was aware that I had really, really moved out of the city and was in a different place entirely. The World no longer applied to us. (Only the gunfire was familiar. We heard a lot of that in the city.)

❧

It was several days before I heard the planes again. This

time they swept low under Red Rock across the valley and disappeared through the gap at Mockingbird Hill. Then they hung a left, one following the other—three of them—and swung around just on the other side of our neighbor with the guns. They headed south, and then an F-16 zoomed low over all of us and tore through the valley and disappeared around Red Rock! I was pumped! I was like a little boy this time. Wifey was mildly annoyed. The neighbor emptied his guns into the woods.

This became normality. We were able to live with both the planes and the shooting. If we had moved in next door to a zoo, we reasoned, we would expect the roar of lions, the trumpeting of elephants, the barking of seals. We had moved into an area targeted by the military as a great place to practice hiding behind mountains below radar detection. Our boys had to be good at it, and they were practicing at our place. No big deal. We are patriots. The shooter? He threw his lead elsewhere. None of it seemed to get away from him and cause trouble. He had already withdrawn himself from the company of others as much as he could. He was a loner, and he had his peccadilloes. The way I figured it, he had done Viet Nam for me personally: he had gone in my place, risked everything while I taught school. I could cut him some slack.

"As long as we're not personally involved, it's cool," said Wifey.

"I'll bet it's a ride, though," I said, "flying low like that, seeing a cliff right outside your window like some Imax movie. That's got to be a great ride."

"You get car sick. Don't hold your breath: the general isn't going to call you up and offer you a ride, let you take the wheel for a while, wave at me here in the yard, then fly off somewhere and plaster the enemy. I know how your fantasies work."

"I didn't..."

"So just forget it. We'll keep our mouths shut, and things will be just fine."

"But..." I argued convincingly.

"Pass the salt, please."

A day came when we noticed that the planes were gone. All planes were gone. High up, on a route between Little Rock and Oklahoma City or Kansas City, or maybe between Houston and Chicago, or New Orleans and Minneapolis, we could usually see planes and contrails. But one day it stopped. The sky was wiped clean. On TV, the towers were falling in New York, and our isolation was over. Mankind, our country, The World, all was suddenly very close to our remote mountain. Our neighbor emptied several guns into the woods *for me* as the huge clouds choked Manhattan on TV.

The View—the tiny farms way down below, the little highway, the distant cliffs and rocks, the hazes and mists, the marks of man and mathematics on the land—seemed more precious than ever. I gazed at all of it, "purple mountained majesty..."—wishing for a huge airplane, free and on the loose in our valley, or miles up, near the floor of outer space, chalking a reassuring, man-made white line. But nothing in the air was moving at all, except for buzzards circling. All thoughts were grim thoughts. I wanted to go out into the woods and empty my own guns—at nothing, but with "extreme prejudice." The absence of airborne men made The View seem unnatural.

"Some of the natives say the planes disturb the chickens and mess with their laying habits," the neighbor lady had said of the planes. "Some think they're spying for the government—like Peeping Toms or CIA people looking for drug factories or pot crops. But most of us are old, and we know about war, and you've got to make sacrifices—even if it's just putting up with low-flying planes."

"Well," I said, "I like them now. It's a little excitement. A reminder."

"Just remember: they're ours! And because they're flying here, we'll never have to be worrying about the planes being 'theirs'." The neighbor lady knew about such times.

"Yeah. They're ours. I'll take it."

I remembered, for some reason, sitting on my

grandmother's lap in her darkened living room in Minnesota during an air raid drill during World War II. An air raid drill in a tiny town in the middle of the continent, so far from any enemy that it was a joke. Nobody laughed. We all participated, because all of us were at war—even little kids saving tin foil. And now, with thousands dying in our own country, we were all at war again, old and young, in the embattled cities, and on lonesome mountain tops. Our duty now was to sit still and let our boys fly by, below the radar, and wave gratefully. Or reach out and shake hands! Others would have to submit to intimate searches, long waits, scanning, interrogation, inconvenience, bureaucratic stupidity. Participation for all.

In just a few days, they came again: our boys, rattling our windows, slicing open the valley's clouds, shaving the treetops. We waved and smiled and got goose bumps. And then, in what seemed like only a few more days, it was reported by a network news outfit on TV that a C-130 with nine aboard had crashed in Afghanistan, all hands lost.

"Makes you wonder, don't it?" said the neighbor lady.

"Yeah. I wonder if it was our boys."

"It was. No matter who it was, it was our boys."

Over across the highway and off about a half mile, the rattle of gunfire, almost a salute this time, added solemnity to the rituals of the day. Way off in the hills, far from just about everything, below the radar, we were involved in mankind.

Halloween

All they do down there at that Halloween party is try to scare themselves to death," our chief advisor warned us. "That old fool down there is part stupid and part crazy."

"Now, now. I've heard he's part genius and part grandfather—and all fun. Guess we better check him out." I was finally skeptical about the neighbor lady's advice, and this time I was resisting.

"Down there" was a deep valley a few miles south of our diggings. We were poised high on the rim of the Big Creek Valley, but the Halloween party was to take place at the very bottom of what seemed a deeper valley a few mountains away— an ancient place where pre-historic man and Native Americans and early white settlers all had taken a turn. There were rumors of everything from Bigfoot sightings to alien abductions in modern days, remnants of a whole community a couple of generations back, and strange rock formations influenced by probably the Indians and later by teenaged vandals. The party's host, his soup, and his party were well-known for miles around.

"We have been invited by friends we cannot refuse, and we are going to the party," I told the neighbor lady.

"Unless the weather gets bad," said Wifey. "I'm not going down there if it's raining."

"Good luck!" said the neighbor lady, stalking away into her kitchen.

❧

I could tell that Wifey did not really want to go to the party.

I considered myself way past caring about Halloween parties, but friends in town told us this was a bash not to be missed. We were committed to the experience. Besides, I reasoned, it will do us good: shake us up a little, enrich our lives, that sort of thing. "Won't hurt us a bit," I think I remember saying.

The day arrived quickly, and the weather cleared up nicely. At 4:30 in the afternoon, the sun was shining, the autumn colors were spectacular, and Wifey and I were following our friends down the steep road into the abyss.

Oh, we had squirmed. We had, in fact, cancelled. We did not like to go out at night; we did not know the host of the party; we did not wish to subject our poor pickup to that dirt road; we were on a diet and did not need to get into a pig-out; we did not trust the weather; we weren't getting any younger; whine whine whine; yada yada yada. We were just lazy, and that's how you get old. But we felt bad about slighting our friends, and we went to the party.

Wifey always drives. It is not that she is a particularly great driver, but she is a terrible passenger. And I am too lazy to fight the problem, and fighting the problem with Wifey is never worth the pain. And so Wifey drove, following our friends in their passenger car with our pickup truck, down and down and ever deeper and deeper into the strange valley. It was slow going, and we were certain twice that we were all lost. Once, we met an on-coming vehicle, and it was difficult, even in daylight, to sidle past. But, Wifey managed, slowly and carefully.

Shortly after five, however, we were on level ground at the bottom of the valley (all swathed in wonderful fall colors), and we made a sudden right turn, and we were there—in a swarm of off-road vehicles and trucks and sturdy cars, in a big yard all decorated for Halloween.

In a few minutes, we found ourselves among familiar faces and feeling most welcome. We met many strangers, too, and our host. He turned out to be sort of the patriarch of the modern version of the valley: he had a huge personal family and legions of friends, and he was a catalyst for artists, musicians, craftsmen, and miscellaneous characters. And he threw a hell of a party. We were able to pry out of him short anecdotes about the rigors of living in so secluded a place. He was amusing and colorful.

There was a pig-out, of course: a pot-luck feast, highlighted by the host's excellent and famous soup. We commandeered a picnic table, and soon about eight of us were talking about UFOs and Bigfoot monsters, lions and tigers and bears, and the ghosts of the valley's ancestry that must be just beyond the tree-lines all around, watching. (Yeah, we were there to scare ourselves. It was Halloween.) And we ate! Wifey and I sinned grievously—and merrily. And repeatedly! Everybody did, young and old.

And there were indeed young people present. We hadn't seen young people since the city! Even when we went into town for entertainment, it was Branson, and it was gray. But this night, a whole simultaneous party raged away for the kiddies; the teenagers lurked around the toughest-looking trucks, looking tough themselves—all pierced and stapled and tattooed and "Gothed out"; parent-types seemed to gravitate toward the large campfire and trance-like introspection; the older folks went into the house where it was warm. There were little knots of people here and there all over the scene. We knocked around with all of them, but finally settled in the warm house where the music was being played.

And all over the "campus," the work of our zany host was evident. There was a coffin with a pop-up corpse, a witch that heard what you said and talked to you, a fleet of ghosts flying through the air around the yard, a little graveyard wherein were buried Care, Worry, Pain, and Sorrow—R.I.P. on their tombstones. Rocks had teeth, tree stumps swallowed little boys, walls had eyes. As it got dark, the place was a carnival of frightful fun. Somewhere a wolf howled. That was probably real. The cold, clammy air added to the atmosphere. We do indeed enjoy scaring ourselves.

With the gray-headed mob in the main house, in the great room where one could imagine generations of festive family activities, a circle of musicians flailed away: twelve or so instruments and many voices of various flavors and qualities, our host playing lead guitar. Traditional country and gospel music filled the warm, relaxing air. The décor was Modern Goblin, trimmed in pumpkin. On the walls, the family ancestors looked on with approval from old tin-types, sepia tones and black and whites, studio re-touch jobs, and laser prints: old pioneers and Bay Watch babes—all in the family.

Wifey and I took our places as observers. Wifey was able to talk to her friend a little, but I was unable to communicate with my friend because he can't hear and I don't listen. The ladies said so, so it must be true.

"Great music," I yelled at him.

"No. I say we bomb the hell out of Iraq."

"I say, the music is really great. Traditional. The real thing."

"Well, I sure liked his soup."

❧

The sentiments of some of the country songs seemed desperate. "It's a good thing you're a bad thing, 'cuz I've got it bad for you," and "If you turn up at my place, I'm gonna turn you down," and the equally paradoxical "I screwed up when I turned you down, but you were right when you left" made me want to check my own hearing. And there were work songs: "If you just came to watch the clock, I've got no time for you." All in good fun. It made me want to be a song writer.

❧

Outside, the little ones terrified each other, leaping out of shadows in their weird costumes and masks, and exploring the dark out-buildings with little flashlights. Later, there was a hay ride that they wouldn't let old guys like me go on. I tried. I don't know what the teenagers did, but they did it in the dark, whatever it was. I had known them for 37 years as a teacher, and now I could not imagine their lives. I was getting old. But it was good to see them.

Time passed, and a light mist developed on the floor of the valley. I detected it while I was visiting the campfire bunch, and I went into the great room and tried to spirit Wifey away. I cited weather complications, and she bought it. We said our reluctant good-byes and thanked our host and headed for the pickup. That took some time, and it took another half hour to get past the group at the campfire. It was a great party.

The new windshield wiper blades were on the dashboard of the truck, right where I had left them. I was going to put them on later. The old ones did their best in those first few minutes, and we pulled out of the yard and headed up the road. At first, we could see fine. We were glad we had left early. There was not much rain: just enough to require wipers. Fortunately, we observed, there was no fog.

Actually, you cannot call a cloud fog. Our host had mentioned that earlier. As we slowly climbed along the terrible road—the road infamous for creating flat tires, as our host had mentioned at the party—we entered a heavier mist. Our low beams handled it well, and we pushed onward. And upward. After a few minutes, we entered the lower levels of what you cannot call fog. We rose into the heart of the cloud shortly after that: the "cloud wall" mentioned by our host in one of the anecdotes we had pried from him at the party. The cloud wall that could not be penetrated by headlights. The opaque cloud wall.

We were familiar with the cloud routine, of course. We had looked out at it many times from the safety of our house: thick, choking, impenetrable; and many times we had pledged to one another that we would never willingly go out driving in that soup. It was like a huge wet mop wrapped around us—slobbery and all-encompassing. It was like looking into a milk bottle. They don't have milk bottles anymore, but I know what I'm talking about here.

Those dirt roads don't have center lines—or centers, for that matter. We had heard stories about people on their hands and knees in front of their cars on that road, looking for a clue as to where exactly they were. Of course, we were skeptical until that night .

But Wifey inched along, able to see only a few feet of road in front of us. She did not seem happy about the un-installed new wiper blades, now that I think about it. She commented on it at the time. Several times, in fact. I offered to get out on the hood and mop the windshield with my shirt as we moved along—perhaps feeling our way with a stick. I offered to walk in front of the car in the rain and signal the safest route, avoiding the sharpest stones, if I could find them. I offered to ride back in the box, like cargo. Anything. But then an owl came out of the night and whapped into our windshield and wrapped itself around our radio aerial and hung there dead, looking at us. The rain intensified at about that time, so the blood was taken care of. I decided not to get out of the vehicle needlessly.

Our five years of mountain training kicked in right at the critical moment. The rock slide was actually fortuitous: I loaded a few of the heftiest ones into the truck, clearing the road and affording us much more traction. (I was able to wrestle them up the front of my body and nudge them over the edge into the box.) The big white animal in the road turned out to be not Bigfoot but a cow, and our lights helped it get off the road, with me pushing a little. The downed tree was lying in a wide spot in the road—nearly wide enough for vehicles to meet—and it was small enough that I could swing most of it to the side., putting my pitiful shoulder into it. When the wind kicked up, we recognized the black walnut barrage immediately and experienced only minor, temporary terror—even kept the ones that fell into the truck's box with the rocks. When we thought we were lost, we used gravity to guide us, for everywhere we wanted to go was up. The thirty-foot rock wall on the left helped us, too, and the drop-off to the right was recognizable: a dark void, echoless, ignorant.

And there was music in our hearts. "This little light of mine, I'm gonna let it shine..." to the rhythm of the disintegrating windshield wipers. "I'll fly away, oh lordy, I'll fly away..." whenever we got near the brink on the right shoulder.

"I once was lost, but now I'm found, was blind but now I see…" as we recognized something in the gloom. Hymns and gospel.

And prayers, too. "Yay, though I walk through the valley of the shadow of death…" and "Thy will be done…" as despair approached. And a constant litany of, "Oh, my God!" and "Help me, Jesus!" It was a religious experience.

And poetry. "Two roads diverged in the yellow wood, and I screwed up and took the one less traveled. And that has made all of the difference!"

And drama. "Come, thick night, and pall thee in the dunnest smoke of hell…" and "Come, seeling night, scarf up the tender eye of pitiful day…" as the cloud wrapped us up and tucked us away "I have almost forgot the taste of fears: The time has been, my senses would have cool'd to hear a night-shriek…" when the truck let out a scream of protest or the tires howled. Too many years of teaching *Macbeth*.

We were ready. We were willing to pull off the road and simply stop, but there was no place to pull off the road. The true path was ahead, and up, probably. We were willing to stop and change drivers, but by then it was too steep to risk stopping. And we were familiar with the various effects achieved by road maintenance crews: the washboard effect, the moonscape effect, the plowed field effect—we were trained for all of that. Even the stretch of crumbled acorns, where there was absolutely no traction, was familiar. And we knew when we saw a strange light above us that it was just an on-coming vehicle hurtling down on us from above—not a UFO. We knew enough to stop and pull over as far as possible and pray with our eyes shut: slammed shut! We were mountain folks now, and we understood.

And we grew. I was able to move rocks and trees larger than I ever thought possible, and I think I lifted the truck once while pushing it. The work warmed me and stopped my teeth from chattering excessively. Wifey was able to employ skills she had gleaned inadvertently along the way: she could manufacture a sense-making picture out of scant details in the gloom, an ability probably picked up on the hundreds of occasions when she had lost or forgotten her glasses. We could hear engine sounds that we had not noticed before, and there were fumes that tasted rubbery and sulfurous. All of our senses sharpened, and we were terrified—genuinely terrified. The party had been unnecessary!

After what seemed like hours, a red stop sign presented itself rather abruptly, and we knew that we were on top, at the highway, practically safe. Home, sanctuary, scotch and valium were just nineteen murky miles away. Our tires still had air in them, and one of our headlights was still shining. Halloween was nearly over, and we were still alive and still married.

Our cargo of muddy rocks had been washed by the torrents of rain, and the water had drained out the back as we climbed the steep mountain. I was later able to incorporate the rocks in a retaining wall at home. The whole truck got a nice wash as we tore through the clouds on the highway and at last made it to our heavily cloaked driveway. The left rear tire gave one last hiss as we hit the ground and scampered into the house. We made it home!

The whole thing inspired me to install the new wiper blades, replace a headlight, check into some new tires, and get the truck winterized. The knees were out of my jeans—partly from straining in the muck and mire and partly from the praying. After my clothes dried, I was able to burn them out back in the trash barrel. I warmed my hands over the flames, and that was festive, too. There were no significant consequences of the pig-out, for we burned a lot of calories there along that road—when you stop and think about it. Good party!

Also, we needed the rain. And I think the cats got that owl.

Apparently, these things are all arranged, including the terrifying, strenuous experiences. All we have to do is pay attention.

Hot Water

It was a plumbing problem, most likely, and not one stemming from the fact that the Senior Citizens' Center was a former mortuary. It was something inside the wall: some routing problem that nobody seemed to be able to fix. Fact was, though, that all of the water in the men's room was hot: the Cold tap, the Hot tap, the john, and the urinals—all hot.

"Water heats up too much and she backs up into all the pipes," one old timer theorized.

"It's simple. A moron could see it. The pipes head to the wrong place," another ventured. "Place ain't plumbed right."

"Just a bad idea to make a funeral parlor into anything else! Angry spirits in these walls, I'm tellin' yuh." (I liked that one.)

"Naw. Whole thing's a conspiracy to keep plumbers coming back here and pickin' up a paycheck. You seriously think a real plumber couldn't fix it in an hour?" Indeed, plumbers came and went, but the problem remained.

On a normal day, during a normal visit (lunch), a man might encounter the warmth of the men's room about once—and he would notice! But the water had a chance to cool after it reached the site, and the fewer the flushes the cooler the water. As one old boy said, though, that cuts both ways. (Sort of a new natural law.) It was possible to encounter cool or lukewarm water, but usually, the water was hot.

A man, especially an older man, hesitates to enter into a conversation about such things with women, and women ran the Senior Citizens' Center.   "Uh...ma'am?"   one   could feature some old boy saying, "I have prostate problems, and I really hate to work myself up into a sweat when I'm spending my five minutes at the urinal." It wouldn't happen. Older men are polite. Or tired.

Some of the old coots had lived in days when restrooms were rather Spartan, too. And I was one of those old coots. This john was indoors, thank you, and we hated to seem ungrateful.

And they had a cute little sign on the wall in that restroom, too, that, in crude poetry, encouraged men to pay attention to their marksmanship. Some guys were offended—not by the crudeness, but by the implication, the insult. They had been doing this all of their lives, after all, and they were Seniors now! Experts. Still, nobody complained.

The first time I personally encountered the hot water, I went into denial. I was willing to believe that it was my imagination, or that I was over-reacting, or that this was something they did for old people in the mountains, or that, like many things I ran into in this new world of Retirement and Senior Citizenship, this thing simply could not be happening. I quietly checked it out with my friend Double-Dog Darrell, though, and he assured me that it was true: we had hot water, and we had it bad.

No real harm was being done, it could be argued: nobody had scalded anything precious or vital (that anyone mentioned out loud); the Center's plumbing had not harmed any of the men's plumbing; warm beats the heck out of cold, especially in winter; among "geezerkind," "warm" means "alive," nobody had totally freaked out, so far; yada, yada, yada. We became inured to the phenomenon, and most quit mentioning it at all.

The Area Senior Men's Nine Ball Tournament came to town one February day, and pool enthusiasts from all over the district came to play. The place would be turned over to the men, and it would be a festive occasion. The tables would be lit up and clattering from early morning till well into the afternoon, and there would be refreshments: plenty of snacks and plenty of drink. (Not alcohol, mind you: this is a dry county we're talking about here! Alcohol is private, and Nine Ball is a game of concentration and precision.)

Pool was not my cup of tea, but I was on hand to see how some of our local players fared. Unlike Professor Harold Hill, I considered the hours I spent with a cue in my hands to be laughable. I had shot a game or two with some of the boys, after Wifey had challenged them on my behalf, but I attended the pool tournament as a spectator, loyal to our Center's team. And I was curious about how things in that rest room might turn out. I maneuvered to a good vantage point, and I settled in.

The first round or two went off without a hitch. A few of our local players advanced and looked good in there. I had to admire some of the no-nonsense, high-tension gamesmanship, and I was pleased to see that the competition was good natured.

But I was more interested in the restroom traffic, because I like real drama. When one of our guys visited the toidy (just a few feet from the pool room), nothing was said. There were little winks for those who were tuned in, but nothing overt. We "locals" were all in on this together. (Besides, it was February, and it was cold outside, and any warmth was appreciated. You reach a certain age when you cherish the little gifts.) Soon the traffic to the john was brisk, and you could say that, as the tournament heated up, so did the men's room. Each flush brought hotter water.

It wasn't long before a rather worried looking little fellow from Western Grove came into the pool room, and his glasses were fogged over. "My God," he said, "They's hot water in yer peein' trough in thar! And they's live steam all in the air."

"Must be yer imagination," Old Elmer, one of our boys, said. "Never noticed anythin' like that before. Y'awl sure y' ain't runnin' a fever?"

"Oh, yeah. You could be sick. West Nile Virus fer sure. You

don't look good at all," one of our other wags chided. " Y o u could be havin' and attack o' the vapors!" a guy with a white pony tail offered.

There was chuckling, but a few of the other visiting players went to investigate. Our guys didn't blink. Pool players like to needle and kibitz a little: it's part of the fun. All concentrated on the game, quite innocently.

Presently, four men with drooping hair and steamed glasses entered the pool room together and, almost simultaneously, as if choreographed, they took off their glasses and took out their shirt tails and proceeded to shine their lenses. Behind them, a cloud loomed and then crept into the room. It was like morning on the mountain.

Naturally, there was a howl of laughter now. Live steam will do that to a pool tournament. The cloud moved in and settled low over Table #2 and threatened to shut down the game. "Must be ghosts," said one old boy. "This was a funeral parlor, you know. Lots of spirits floatin' around." Someone else commented that it finally looked like a pool hall in there. In the confusion, at Table #1 Old G. W. ran a whole rack in the Nine Ball game, and our boys forged ahead!

"Y'awl kin laugh if'n yuh want to, but you boys have got a problem in that thar toilet. One old boy is lost in the fog in thar, and with all this noise, we cain't talk him out."

"Tell him to get down on his knees," said White Pony Tail. "It ain't as thick down there. You boys got to learn to adapt."

Well, Old G.W. won the tournament. He would have won it anyway, even without the "water hazard." Everybody had sort of a wilted look, though: there was not one crease left in one pair of pants at the end of the day. It was February in the pool room, but it was a hot August night in the men's restroom.

One of the Western Grove boys had a good idea, too. "Y'awl ought have lobster at yer next tournament. You've got a great place fer cookin' 'em."

❧

I decided to get more serious about pool. Someday. And someday, they would fix that plumbing, too. But it would spoil things.

The County Meeting

A single tidbit of new information or a chance meeting can change the way you think; indeed it can start you thinking when your mind has lain dormant for an embarrassing period of time. And it can happen in the best of neighborhoods, even ones you have personally trodden flat: places you have mindlessly passed by without thinking. And it happens especially if you tend to overanalyze things.

One fateful autumn day, on the way up the mountain, just a few hairpin curves and several layers of rock south of the village, I became aware of a situation that had so far escaped my notice.

I had passed this way many times, day and night, going to and from the village on the urgent errands of my new life in the hills. The highway I was on was the "new" Scenic Byway Seven, and I came upon a crossroads I had always considered insignificant before. What was different this time was that I had just learned that this was the junction at which Old Highway Seven, a gravel road, forked off to the left and slid around the side of Round Top Mountain, well downhill.

I had heard of Old Highway Seven many times, but I had never known that this was it. It was like the Bottomless Pit I had heard about—and like hidden waterfalls and enchanted rock formations I had never visited on purpose, but had heard enough about to believe strongly (or suspect strongly). The new highway slanted up the side of the mountain, very steeply, to Scenic Point, and then off down the ridge to the South, put there, obviously, so that the tourists would have a chance to get up there and look down and gasp in wonder at the Buffalo River Canyon. Old Seven tunneled through heavy forest, right below the new highway, and was now nearly overrun by vines and berry brush: an intriguing road, perhaps, but not a touristy place at all. I had been there while lost one afternoon, but I had no clue that it was Old Seven! I was just lost, again.

But as I reached the junction this time, I was so struck by the general layout of the place that I pulled over and stopped. I had never thought it out before.

On the left side of the highway right at the fork was the County Fair Grounds complex, where once a year the locals would gather to show what could be done in the area (arts, crafts, agriculture, etc.). Young people got started there, and older ones had an opportunity to show what they had left. On the right side at that fork in the road was the county's conservation office. The two facilities seemed to fit together nicely, preserving, conserving, saving. The old and the new at the juncture of the old and the new highway! Hmmmm.

Just ahead on the right was the county's dump and the re-cycling center. Here, if you were through with it or had worn it out, you could throw it away, and somebody might be able to salvage its essence: give it one last chance, save it. It seemed ironic that this set-up would be placed just there. Junk at the junction, but more preserving, conserving, saving.

And across the highway from that was the run-away truck ramp, where vehicles whose brakes had failed had one last chance to stop before plummeting into the town or over the edge into the abyss, or into the face of a stone cliff. It was a trough of deep, loose gravel that would mire down an out-of-control truck, and save everybody, and save the truck from becoming junk!

Had someone actually planned all of this? I had to think about it.

At the fork itself, just off the main thoroughfare, there was a large, reasonably level, paved apron: sort of a diving platform for Old Seven—or, if you were coming out of the fair grounds or Old Seven, it was what you grabbed onto: an entry ramp, perhaps, dry land, safety at last, a foothold in the modern world. (When you made it to pavement from almost any secondary mountain road in the area, you needed a spot like this to stop, give thanks, count your blessings, and maybe check your tires.) I was paused there for a different reason now: I was studying the great enigma, the irony, the puzzle of the whole juncture.

At such "King's X" areas or neutral zones throughout the county, you would often see a little knot of pickup trucks gathered for what Double-Dog Darrell once informed me was facetiously called a "county meeting" by some local wags. It was common for locals to pull off the highway at such spots, drop an end gate or drape themselves over the hood of a chosen pickup, and parley the issues: purely on impulse, with no prior planning, no malice of forethought, target-of-opportunity sort of thing. Outsiders (and I was one) would slow down, rubberneck a little, and wonder what was so important, what had caused this little confab, and why there! (Tourists probably said, "Have these people no cell phones?") How quaint, right?

This was a juncture for other familiar local phenomena, now that I thought about it. It was the level where my ears popped on the trip up or down the mountain. For other people it may have happened at other elevations, but for me, that was the spot: my own personal Eustachian station! And when we were in a blind fog at our house, chances were that we could drive down to the village, and about at this level, drop under the cloud into clear visibility. Going up, this was often where we would enter the cloud, say good-bye to reality, and be forced to feel our way home, slowly, carefully.

Sometimes it was winter up at our house and spring or autumn down in the village—starting at about this point: snow above, rain below! Sometimes it was ice below and ice and snow above. But usually, this was the elevation where things changed.

High above on the right stood Round Top (Judea Peak

in the old days), the dominating landmark, its ghostly peak sometimes lost in a cloud, as it was once in the forties when a military plane crashed into it (famous local tragedy). Nearby, downhill, was the site of another nightmare: when a busload of people went over the side (another famous local tragedy). Probably not connected, I decided. But the proximity! I worried.

This place was significant, I was prepared to insist: it was pivotal, symbolic, bothersome, spooky. I wondered if ancient man had thought so—Native Americans, maybe: The Osage, The Cherokee, the Choctaw, the Kickapoo. I had read about hermits and other societal drop-outs who had lived wild in the vicinity. I had the feeling that this place had always been a crossroads. If there were more people around, there would certainly be a burger joint, a pizza parlor, a chicken outfit. I brooded.

ॐ

While I was standing by my pathetic pickup, a newer, cleaner pickup pulled in beside me. It was Doc Schullenheimer, a friend of mine from down at the Senior Center, a neighbor.

"Some kind of problem?" he asked, rolling down his window.

"Naw. I'm just thinking about this place."

He looked at me with his diagnostic eye. He was indeed a doctor, retired now and into volunteer work, like many in the hills. (He told me that he retired because his name would not fit on the prescription forms.)

"Well, if you need any help, I have connections at the dump," he told me with mock sincerity. "I happen to know the management. I work there, you know."

"Yeah. I know."

"I am plugged into all the power sources over there. I don't like to brag, but I can get you almost anything: cans, wire, muck, mire. Just say the word." Twinkle in the eye—mock smugness.

Doc and I had spent time together at the dump/recycling center during one of his volunteer Saturdays. We had accounted for $63 worth of junk while I was there, and he had stayed longer. I had enjoyed his dumpside manner when he answered the phone: "County Dump, Trash Can speaking."

"No, really. I was just thinking that this was a very ambiguous junction—a juncture of cosmic significance."

"Oh. Well, you don't need a doctor, you need Double-Dog Darrell or some other local philosopher. Me, I am into aluminum salvage these days. I do remember a little brain surgery."

ॐ

At that moment there was a terrible roar, and down the Old Seven tine of the fork, in a huge cloud of dust and debris, the terrible Hummer of Moose Vandergrift came tearing toward us, all four wheels digging and flinging rocks and dirt in all directions. I was not terrified because Moose was my friend; Doc knew him because he had removed a thorn from the big fellow's paw some years back. When the wind blew away the debris cloud, Moose was standing by his camouflaged vehicle like a rogue elephant during must: stamping, trumpeting, bugging his eyes. Awesome! Other than his huge overalls, he had nothing but his fur to protect him from the elements.
"Grnmph flrngk gromple shroquel mfhrnkp!" Moose snarled as he slammed a fist down on his monstrous machine. It was a blow that would have crushed a lesser vehicle.

"He says he's angry," said Doc.

"I know. We have worked together," I muttered to Doc. "What have we done?" I asked Moose.

"Raphcl gnashe rassle frass munklebeut frmmnnllg?" he screamed.

"Oh, this is no meeting, Moose! Nobody called a meeting. This just happened. I was stopped here, and Doc showed up..."

Moose moved over to me, clouted me on the shoulder, and laughed, I believe. "Rnglnthw frungloppen drvlngt," he said.

"He was just kidding," said Doc.

"Yeah, I got it. Let's humor him. Meanwhile, how are you with collar bones?" I had pain. Real pain.

ॐ

Another pickup truck pulled off new Scenic Byway Seven, and another came up out of the fair grounds. Both parked with our group, forming a formidable clump of pickup trucks. So now a fighter pilot (retired) and a young auctioneer joined the group.

"My God," I said out loud, "I have inadvertently spawned a County Meeting!"

Both the fighter pilot and the auctioneer wanted to know who had called the meeting and why, and I tried to explain. But it was hopeless. There was nothing for it but to proceed. It wasn't long before we were all at work on The Economy, the Iraq situation, Terrorism in general, and gun control issues. It was agreed that, if Washington would listen to us, we could clear things up in a hurry. We later talked about women, insulated coveralls, chain saws, and leather gloves. We drew maps, charts, and graphs in the dust on the hoods of the trucks; we pulled out guns from our gun racks; we even compared WalMart receipts, oil additives, fan belts. It was a great meeting.

A UPS truck stopped by, and the guy in the brown outfit got Moose to deliver a package for him—way back in the wilderness where a sane UPS man would not go, but no trick at all for a Hummer. The High Sheriff Himself showed up, too, and passed out election leaflets, and he advised us to toss out a few flares if the meeting lasted until after dark. Doc's friends from the dump brought over some cokes. Passers-by slowed, gawked, waved, honked.

Naturally, I thought about the junction, the meeting, the whole rendezvous—for a long time after that; and I have to admit it: I was perplexed. I became convinced that there were places in the Universe where lines crossed, where worlds and dimensions and perspectives converged: gates, perhaps, portals! And I concluded that this magic place, down there by the dump and the fair grounds, at the end of the run-away truck ramp, was probably such a place. Then a guy on TV convinced me that I was just not getting enough calcium. I'm better now.

Poached Squirrel

Wifey's fresh-baked bread had lured our oldest new friend to our table, and we were unashamed. Mr. Hooper was a master gardener, and he grew tomatoes half as big as a human head—and bushels of tender green beans, bales of spinach, plump radishes and potatoes, any vegetable he pleased. And wonderful strawberries. He fed many elderly friends, delivering produce to their doors, or meeting them on neutral ground for "sharing." "I've spoilt 'em all," he told us.

Mr. Hooper was well into his upper eighties, and he could tell you about World War II as if it happened yesterday. He had been in the Pacific with the navy. On this occasion, however, he ate bread and talked about soil and weather and seeds and fertilizers. We baited him. In gardening, he was where we wanted to be. He made it clear that the bread was his focal point, but we steered him as well as we could: How do you grow things in these hills?

After we had picked his brain and taken notes about next year's garden ["I start mine fifteen minutes after Christmas," he had told us], someone told a story—probably a forgettable one, since I have forgotten. (Probably me, now that I think about it.) But then it was Mr. Hooper's turn.

"Well, now let me tell one," he said, getting his hands up on the table to make the story grow. "I ever tell you-uns about the Poached Squirrel?"

"Poached squirrel?" said Wifey. "I don't think so." I could tell she was thinking about cooking.

"Well, it was The Depression," he began. "We was down

along the river, me and my buddy, a-livin' in a shanty we had
built outa everything we could steal: used old billboard signs
from along the road as sheeting in the roof, logs outa the woods,
old boards from broke-down chicken coops, and like that. We
was jist a-squattin' there in them woods. But we had learnt that
we could kill and dress out a few squirrels and make about a
quarter apiece on 'em in town. Back then, that was money.

"So, one day me and my buddy kilt up about twenty or so
squirrel, dressed 'em out, and put 'em in a shotgun can—tall
straight-sided can used mostly fer milk—with a little water, and
stretched some kinda cover over the top of it, and headed fer
the road to hitch into town.

"Now, you could see through that stuff we had a-coverin'
the top of that bucket. Squirrels was out-o-season, and it was
illegal to sell game at all, but folks in town was a-starvin' fer
some good meat, and this was cheap, and nobody cared. The
woods was full o' squirrel.

"Anyway, we gets us out by the road and we sticks out our
thumbs, and first thing you knowed, we was in this fella's car a-
headin' fer town. About four mile." With his hands, he formed
the whole picture for us, shaping each unfamiliar object into
something we could understand.

"We jist hopped in that car without a-lookin' at who it was.
A ride was a ride, and we had done enough walkin' a-huntin'
them squirrel. Well, we gets in there, and I puts that big shotgun
can o' squirrel meat between my feet—me a-settin' in front and
my buddy in the back seat. Model-A Ford. Then I gets a look at
the driver."

"Game Warden," I blurted out, trying to get ahead of him.
I hate people like me. I got a swift kick under the table from
Wifey, and she was right to do it. I shut up.

"Well, he had some uniformy-lookin' pants on, and a cap
that had some kinda writin' on it, but he looked straight ahead
and I couldn't get a good look. His shirt was jist a shirt—not
like any kinda uniform. But you know I was a-thinkin' what you
was a-thinkin': Game Warden—or somebody that could run me

in fer shootin' them squirrel out-o-season. So I kindly covered that shotgun can best I could.

"Well, right away he starts in on me. 'What you-uns got in that bucket, son?' And I started a-lyin' right there. 'Them's eggs,' I told him. 'My old momma sent me to town to sell off some eggs.'" Mr. Hooper put on an innocent face as he portrayed himself as a young liar. "I went on about my poor old momma, a-raisin' them eggs to eke out a livin'—and me a-helpin' out all I could by a-takin' 'em to town. We're about to walk through our shoes. Our britches is so thin you can see through 'em,' I told that man. My buddy in the back jist keeps shut.

"'Sure would like some of them eggs,' he says to me. Well, I about turned purple right there, and I knowed I had to cook up a good one fast. 'Oh, momma's got these all sold in town. We got us a contract. I gotta deliver these eggs to *certain* folks! These eggs ain't fer sale to jist anybody.'

"Well, he gets a twinkle in his eye, and I know who he is fer sure. He's the law, I'm jist sure, and he's out to trap me. All the way to town he's a-workin' on me. 'How much you take fer them eggs?' he says. 'I bet I could give you a nickel more'n folks in town. I shore do want some o' them eggs. Nice fresh ones, I bet. Yup, I would please my wife to no end if'n I could come home with some of them eggs.' No matter what I said, he come back with, 'I shore do admire them fresh eggs.'

"And I did some powerful lyin', too. I said, 'These eggs is not fer sale. My old momma would kill me stone daid if'n I didn't get 'em to the folks she said. She'd get real mad. My old daddy run off, and I got to be dependable. I'm a-doin' all I can do around the place, but I got to honor my promise to my own mother. Y'awl kin understand that.' And I told that man I don't know what all, tryin' with my lies to appeal to his decent, Christian side. But it was all lies, ever bit of it, because my old momma was already passed over at that time. Me and my buddy was a-batchin' it out in the woods, that's all. Narry an egg on the place!

"Well, I don't know when it was that he figgered out I was a-lyin', but he kept on a-askin' questions, and I kept on lyin'. 'Storm took the house onct a while back, and we had to scratch together a shanty...Momma's come down with sumthin' and needs medicine...Critters got our garden...All we got's our chickens...We got to stand by our customers...' I never did so much bald-faced lyin' in four miles of road in my life. I got to lyin' so bad that I begun to believe I actually had eggs in that bucket! Fer a while there, I was considerin' sellin' them eggs, too. But all I had was dead squirrel! And he keeps on a-pumpin' me. Just wouldn't quit. I gets sight of my buddy in the back seat and he jist rolls his eyes and shakes his head.

"Then, by and by, we gets into town. By that time, I'm shiverin' like a dog passin' shingle nails, and it's not hot out, I'm jist nervous. And 'bout the time I think he's a-gonna let me out, he pulls up right in front of the courthouse—'tween that and the county jail. 'Oh, Lordy!' I thinks to myself, 'We're doomed. We're gonna set in jail when he sees these poached squirrel.' Now I was hotter'n a depot stove—drippin' sweat, and real uncomfortable." Old Mr. Hooper rolled his eyes and put his expressive hands into prayer configuration, and trembled a little.

"But I takes my bucket and I gets outa that car, somehow. My buddy gets outa the back. And we jist stand there and wait fer it to happen, all contrite and whipped. And, sure 'nuff, the man gets outa his car and steps up on the walk-way with us.

"And then he jist falls on his knees a-howlin' and a-cacklin' and a-laughin' like a hyena. He gets right down on his knees, I tell yuh, and he 'bout dies laughin' right there. Just had conniptions! Me and my buddy was confused, but we kindly chuckled and nudged each other a little.

"'I never did see so much lyin' in my life,' the man says. 'I been all over the hills, but I never seen so much lyin' so quick. You take the cake. I ain't the law, son. How much you chargin' fer them squirrel?'

"I said twenty-five cents apiece, and we made our first sale."

Wifey and I giggled and applauded a little, and I thought about my own squirrel hunting days, but I had no story like Mr. Hooper's . I was born just after The Depression and just before The War. My stories were tamer.

"I ever tell you-uns about what happened at the swimmin' hole? It's not fer mixed company, but I can tell it another way since they's a lady present—who can bake such wonderful bread!"

"How about a nice piece of pie!" offered Wifey.

"Well now," said Old Hooper, "they's only two kinds of pie I like—hot pie and cold..."

Wild Persimmons

From the beginning, I had suspected that something terribly metaphorical was going on with the whole persimmons scene. Here was a fruit that grew wild on medium-sized trees, plentiful and beautiful and plump—moist and sumptuous as a berry, but apple-shaped and golden and about the size of a ping-pong ball or slightly smaller—and it was largely ignored. In November, after the leaves had fallen, the juicy little rascals clung to the branches of their trees in great numbers, undisturbed, it seemed, by birds or other animals or man.

I knew there was a catch. Perhaps nocturnal animals would call for them some night. (There are red berries out there that all disappear on one critical day; the birds know the day!) I did some checking. I found out that possums liked wild persimmons, and that deer and bear would eat all they could reach. I never personally witnessed any of that. I suspected that there was something wrong with the fruit, but that maybe some animals ate persimmons with impunity, or just didn't care about the consequences. Different animals have different tastes.

But for humans, I discovered, there were tough rules. If you happened to pick the right orb from the proper twig on the correct branch of the ideal tree on the exact day when the fruit was perfectly ripe, and then penetrate its lovely but treacherous skin in the proper manner, you could pull in a mouthful of the sweetest, thickest pulp imaginable! There would be large flat seeds a-swim in that succulent nectar, but you could get rid of them with no trouble. Yes, the persimmons could be a wonderful treat: free for the plucking. Dizzying pleasure and nourishment, free. It appealed to me.

But if you made one mistake of technique or timing, you could get a mouthful of alum, your teeth and gums could lose all lubricants, and you could nearly turn inside out, puckering and trying to spit, above and beyond the call of green rhubarb. I found that, from one limb of one tree, I could pick and successfully enjoy three or four of these fantastic delights, and then latch onto one that tasted like a styptic pencil. (Most little boys of my era tried out Dad's styptic pencil one time while snooping in the shaving gear. One time.)

And allowing them to drop naturally, ostensibly at the moment of perfect ripeness, did not help, either—contrary to some advice we had gleaned. Fallen fruit was as undependable as that hanging from the tree. And there was no way of sitting under the tree, waiting them out, and catching them— although, that would be a pursuit that would wipe out some long retirement hours.

"It is unfair," I told our chief advisor, our tiny, white-haired neighbor lady. "It is too random! It is mean."

"It is simple," said the neighbor lady. "You've got to wait until after the first frost."

"Been there, done that," I said. "But the bottom line is, some of them are good and some of them taste like Preparation H. What's up with that?" (I had sampled them repeatedly until the dead of winter, long after the first frost, off the branch and off the ground.)

"You're not doing it right," she said, dismissing me.

I just knew this was going to be one of those "dark-of-the-moon" things, like planting carrots; or, like the old "Don't let the rain hit your tomatoes in July" routine. I would have to wash first—or not wash for a week, probably; or I would have to hold my mouth just right. Maybe it would be an "all in the wrist" technique, or something requiring the independence of the third finger. It would be like cutting those glands out of freshly-killed deer to prevent meat contamination. It was probably like that damned fish that the Japanese eat: if it isn't cooked right, it'll kill you fast!

I even asked Old Hooper, the gardening expert and teller of tales. He was eloquent. "Them things is jist like a old mule," he told me. "A mule will work for you for twenty years jist to get to kick you one time. And then he will make that one time count—kick your butt up around your neck!" I could see the connection: two or three of those persimmons would be utter ambrosia; the next one would make your throat slam shut. Those persimmons were just waiting for the right sucker at the right moment!

Wifey and I cannot tolerate waste. We tried almost everything those first few Novembers, including folk recipes, mountain "lore," and the "conventional wisdom" of the neighborhood—also including chants and incantations, spells and charms, and an extemporaneous sort of pseudo-voodoo that just seemed like a good idea at the time. Once we gathered two or three gallons of those golden beauties, and we mashed them all up in a huge pot and cooked the living soup out of them. (Someone's recipe, mind you.) We mixed in apricot nectar, lemon, lime, Jello, and honey. The resulting product was something that could have been used to stop the flow of blood from a considerable wound, get oil off the garage floor, or putty up wasp holes under the eaves. I know this for a fact. But you couldn't put that stuff in your mouth—not in there with your precious tongue and your teeth and your fragile gums! Still, the pot was cleaned to a bright shine by the terrible substance, and there was a nice smell in the house for a day or so, so all was not lost.

There were rumors of perfectly tasty treats being prepared from these plentiful, beautiful, free fruits, and we could believe them. We were told of the old days and how the pioneers of the area made use of the fruit. Various people used to know this old lady on a nearby mountain who always "had good luck" with wild persimmons. But nobody ever actually brought us a decent dollop of any persimmons-based food product! We would have bought some jams or jellies or cookies. Or the fabled persimmons bars! We were not proud. We would have bid on them at an auction, snagged them at a garage sale, bartered goods or services for them, even accepted them as charity. All idealism and nobility went out the window. But there were no such opportunities. Good thing, too, because we wanted to "harvest" the things and make food out of them—ourselves.

"Git 'em when they're ugly, " Old Hooper told us. "You got to stay away from the skin. They's a layer in there that'll jerk you sideways and make you spit till yer dry as a prune."

"We know about that layer," I said bitterly (no pun intended).

"Way I figger it, this was the forbidden fruit of the Garden of Eden," he said. And I had to agree with that idea. It was the only religious thing I ever heard Mr. Hooper say.

❧

I wondered: what could the wild persimmons be trying to teach us? Certainly they must have purpose. Perhaps they weresomething put there for the lower animals and not for humans at all: indeed, protected from humans by their bitterness. In their tamer form, they were obviously good for something. Such beauty, such color, such symmetry. If life is a learning process, it stands to reason that persimmons must be a learning process, too. Some things can't be learned out of a book or in a lecture hall; sometimes a lesson cannot be given—it must be taken. As a former teacher, it occurred to me that one must pick and taste his own persimmons, because the last thing you would want to do would be to select one of those things off a branch and put it into the mouth of a loved one—or a student. Too chancy. You could make yourself a life-long enemy—or get sued. I worried about it and tried to study the subject.

It also occurred to me that this fruit might indeed have something to do with religion, beyond Old Hooper's theory. The folks on the ridge seemed to pray a lot. Maybe they just picked the damned things and then turned it all over to God. Sounded like a plan to me. And, of course, I suspected that I was over-analyzing again: intellectualizing something that was unworthy of serious thought—trying to solve a problem for myself that was already solved for everybody else—perhaps placing great value on a folly. I did that a lot. But there was mystery attached to the wild persimmons, and that made them irresistible. And I hate it when that happens.

It was all leading somewhere. November rolled round again, and there they were: just lovely—like nuggets hanging there. I had been through a summer of wild raspberries and blackberries and elderberries. We even got into some blueberries, but that was unfair because they were cultivated blueberries. But we picked them ourselves, lending a certain credibility to the act. And now, in deep November, the persimmon harvest was hanging there on the trees: plump, juicy, overly-ripe it seemed to me—at that ugly phase Mr. Hooper mentioned—some of them bursting and oozing their precious nectars. Certainly there must be a way.

I tried a couple of them, and they were wonderful. I tried two more, and they were better! Could the problem be solved? Had the orbiting of the sun and the earth and the stars and the planets finally conspired so that on my tree there would be edible fruit? Were these indeed the treats the locals had sworn were available? I carefully selected Number Five, and I got cocky, I must admit, and I popped it into my mouth. And I thought my eyes were going to bleed. My lips caved in like I had lost my teeth, but my teeth were still in there, chalky and rough. My alveolar ridge turned into a desert, and my buds ran for cover. It was like a generic brand deodorant stick had been run over my gums. The rules had not changed. I wanted to mop out my mouth, with a gunny sack, if necessary.

I had no choice but to bring up the subject once again at the Senior Center down in the village. Wifey would probably kick the living fire out of me under the table, but I had to broach the subject.

Yet another sweet little old lady with blue hair and chains on her glasses was sitting across from us at lunch. Wifey and I had noticed the lady before, shooting pool, I believe; and we sought out her company on this day—networking, one could say. We were having country fried steak, sweet potatoes, peas, and some kind of pudding: not their worst meal by far. Almost festive, in fact. We were admittedly old now, and we were pleased.

"Wild persimmons?" the lady said with a little twinkle in her eye that I should have noticed. "My grandmother and her mother before her lived in these hills, and they passed down to all of us the formula for wild persimmons. Wanna hear it?"

"Please." At last, I had found the answer. Often these things boil down to finding the right person, the right expertise. I just knew we were at the end of the long search. I listened.

"Well, you go out there and you gather up a whole mess of them, and you tear off and throw away those little stars where the stems are, and you put the fruit all in a big pot. Can't be stainless steel—has to be iron."

"Gotcha." I knew it was going to be something simple like that. This chick knew what she was talking about. I watched as she gestured with her wise, experienced hands. It was as if Mother Nature Herself were teaching a lesson.

"Then you put in a cup of water for each gallon of fruit, and you cook it slow for about six hours. Real slow—low heat. Important. Six hours. At that point you strain out the seeds and stuff, and you add a whole mess of sugar, and you let it all cool." It was making sense. I leaned in close. "How much sugar?" Wifey asked.

"A mess! Lots of sugar. Then when it's cooled down, you pop it into the micro..."

"Wait a minute...!" I have instincts. I knew where this was going.

"And you zap it till it's hot again. Then you let it cool, take it out back, and dump it off the cliff; and then you go to Wal-Mart and get you some grape jelly and forget all about the damned wild persimmons, 'cuz they ain't fit for the hogs!"

There was laughter at that point, and people looked at me!

I'm nobody's fool. I've been around a little. I've paid attention. I got the joke. They didn't have microwave ovens or Wal-Mart back when her grandmother was alive. My problem was that I wanted to believe. But here was a lady who had been where I had been. When it came to wild persimmons, we were kindred spirits.

I decided to be content with the three or four good samples that I was courageous enough to nab each November, and to forgive Mother Nature for making the rest so difficult. Most people, after all, have never tasted wild persimmons at all, although I understand they grow in Central Park in New York.

In despair, I also decided to take a traditional Cavalier attitude. I used to know something about poetry, and there was one Cavalier who wrote, "*If she be not so to me, what care I how fair she be?*" Of course, he was talking about women, not persimmon, and I believe he was just kidding himself; still, one thing at least rhymes with the other. I considered it deeply. Maybe I shouldn't have cared about them if the persimmons didn't exactly work for me.

I had to face the sad fact, though, that, come November, I would somehow think I could get it right at last. Maybe with a large-bore syringe of some kind! Maybe I could extract the juices through a small hole in the terrible skin, pull out only the sweetness, invoke the Muse, and win the game. Or, maybe I would just end up with the Wal-Mart grape jelly: something "with a name like..." Never mind.

The Howling

I was never trapped at night by a good book alone. More was involved, but I had no idea what exactly that was—for me. Reading is a discovery process for anyone, but I had to be hit right over the head with the obvious before I recognized the formula for the ultimate experience: getting roped into a real all-nighter with some clever wordsmith. I had no idea that this would include caulking compound.

Tales of the sea, somehow, and unexplained or unexplainable phenomena interested me in early childhood (right after I finished *Mr. Brown's Grocery Truck*); then humorous and satirical works—fictional, ostensibly—inspired me. The Required Reading of my education—The Curriculum—became a necessity of life during my career. I had to take others with me and try to interest them in reading, and that somehow took some of the joy away from my personal reading experiences. So did grading piles of papers. But then I retired, and it was time to rediscover my intellectual hot buttons. And that is when I started hearing the howling.

It was real howling, at the window of the bedroom of our flawed house in the hills. There was something intriguing about giving up the day, flicking off the television after the news and the opening monologue of some night owl talk show, shutting down the flow of the house's business, slipping under a very heavy pile of covers, and getting one-on-one with a juicy book, with the wind howling at that window! When we were engulfed by a thick cloud, the moment was even better. But, you see, I came to believe that the howling was an annoyance rather than a necessity.

Wifey thought so, too. It was an imperfection. Something was wrong with the window, the house itself. How could we put a stop to this racket? Whatever the season, we had wind of some flavor—part of being at a certain elevation, we were certain, and likely having to do with our location in the saddleback of a ridge on the lip of a big valley. During storms, it was , well, excusable; but often, late at night, after all of the house's other noises had shut down, there was a whisper, then a moan, and then the howling: low and subtle sometimes, but often more than that, and occasionally up to a haunting scream. Disturbing. Certainly annoying. It must be preventing sleep, scarring our very souls, contributing to our aging. It was probably fattening, too, or the cause of cancer. Everything else is. Anyway, the howling had to be stopped, most likely.

But the window of that bedroom was high up, and large, of course, for it was located on the downhill side, the side with The View (as if we needed The View to rest and sleep). Getting to the outside of the window required a long ladder or a scaffold—a risky circus act for a sixties-something, bookish person; still, we reasoned, it must be done. And Wifey reasoned that it must be done by me.

"But..." I argued steadfastly.

"After lunch, call the rental place and price the scaffolding."

"But..."

"Or we could borrow Old Hubert's ladder."

Both ladders and scaffolds were eventually brought into "play," and it was altogether satisfying. I set Old Hubert's long ladder's two feet on a large slab of oak in the soft flower bed below the window. No way I was going to allow it to dig into that soft ground! I knew about these things from painting other houses and using other ladders. This ladder was unlike the others, however, in that the aluminum of its right "ankle" was, as it turned out, at an advanced stage of metal fatigue. When that right side folded under, I was squeezing silicone caulk into the places I suspected of howling. It was a slow-motion moment: I rode the ladder across the side of the house, grabbed the lip of the upper deck at the last second, and lowered myself to safety—as if trained in the exercise all my life. Lucky. And exciting, too. The ladder clattered and clanked into a twisted heap. The caulking gun jumped free of the wreck. I was grateful that I was not painting at the time. (I could have befouled that flower bed with Quality Exterior Latex, my accustomed medium.)

That night, as I scanned several do-it-yourself manuals, the window howled some more, and I resolved to beat the thing at its game. I was going to stop that howling, come hell, high water, or Norm Abrams. And Wifey was convinced that she could do something from the inside while I worked on the outside. We made plans, and we assembled equipment in the days that followed. At night I did a little Conan Doyle and Stephen King and even some Thomas Hardy, and Wifey worked on Mary Higgins Clark and Jackie Collins, and the window howled. Bliss.

We hauled home enough rented scaffolding to reach the problem area, I assembled it and braced it and made it safe, and while I injected caulking compound into every nook and cranny I could find on the outside, Wifey stuffed strips of felt into crevices and cracks on the inside. I painted over the sweeping scratch on the side of the house made by the metal ladder during my earlier adventure, and I made yet another attempt at solving my eternal gutter/spout problem. I painted a bit of trim also, and I tidied up the top of the stone job I had done on the lower part of the wall. I even repaired Old Hubert's ladder and made it safe and operative. It was, well, another chapter in the saga of our poor, unsatisfactory house.

That night there was no wind at all. The air lay profoundly dead. No way of checking our progress. A couple of raccoons investigated the scaffolding and peeped in the window of the bedroom, but they lived on the mountain, too, and I enjoyed their visits. (I had read *Killdee House* as a child, a little book about raccoons: one of the books that got me reading in the first place.) They fiddled with an old phone line on the side of the house, though, and I resolved to snip that off the next day. Perhaps it was a string being strummed by the wind. I was thorough.

It would be amusing to report a great blob of frustration at this point, and relate that the howling persisted and that nothing we could do would stop it—that we beat our heads against some glass ceiling in the realm of Fix-It-Yourself—that we got in over our heads and turned the whole thing into a comedy of errors. But no; that was an earlier episode! This time we were completely successful. When the winds picked up again, the howling was gone. Utterly gone.

It took a couple of sessions to figure it all out, but one night I chopped Leno off right after his monologue and went to bed a bit early. I was trying to re-read all of the Sherlock Holmes stories, in chronological order; so I picked up the book and plumped up the pillows and drew in the heavy covers and cocked an ear and listened; then I adjusted the light and shined my glasses and fondled the book mark and opened the book to the next story and re-closed the book and kicked off the covers and took off my socks and listened; then I settled back in and pounded the pillows and re-opened the book and discovered a hangnail and tried to bite it off and stopped myself and closed the book and I listened; then I became preoccupied with my watch and took off my watch and placed it on the table under the lamp and put down the book on the floor by the bed and turned off the light and gave it all up. Then I lay in the dark and I listened. Ridiculous. I turned and twisted and spun the bedding into one huge roll-mop, then extricated myself with some difficulty, and then got out of bed and went back out and watched TV. Conan O'Brien was hopping around on one foot, in drag.

The howling was gone, and I had to acknowledge, that,

right or wrong, logical or plain stupid, that noise had become some sort of necessity—background music, perhaps, for my new life in retirement on the mountain in the unsatisfactory, imperfect house with the magnificent view. It was my "music of the spheres," whether that made sense to anybody else or not. It was part of settling in for the night, part of the reading experience for sure, part of what I was considering harmony in my little universe. It was focus. It was flow. It was part of my inner life, the kindling for my imagination's fires: my muse! It was the bridge between Conan Doyle and Conan O'Brien. It was the voice of my...never mind.

I got over it, mostly, with effort.

I considered ripping out the caulking compound and trying to put back the howling racket, but Wifey helped me stay the impulse. (My other muse.) It would be rash and counter-productive to reverse our extraordinary efforts. We had eliminated an imperfection and made our home a better place. Yada yada yada. And, besides, we had returned the scaffolding a long time ago. Damned stuff costs money.

On the sly, I tried installing a howl in one of the other windows, but such blessings come as gifts, apparently. They come from Nature or God—or both—and you cannot just pop them in and out like light bulbs or computer disks. An imperfection has to be unintentional, after all. And you cannot really "tune" a house, can you? I wanted the house sealed against the coming winter, too: no heat getting out and no cold getting in, and yet, a nice, primitive howl, on cue! I wanted it all. The stuff of dreams. I struggled for several days; then I adjusted to the little sacrifice.

We are just passing through. The lesson of the hills is revealed over and over: we are temporary, and we matter less than we think. Still, The Maker bothered with us, and then He didn't go away. A few nights ago, the window in the computer room took up the howling—a very deep grumbling sort of moan that reaches right in and stirs my soul. It just volunteered, smiling. And I'm not going to fix it. I like it. I can shut my eyes and see moors and heaths and ghost ships and toothy ramparts atop castle walls in long ago, faraway lands. I can conjure up subterranean worlds or cloudy kingdoms or lonesome wastelands where all answers are as vague as my questions. I can ride the arm of a windmill and be flung down into the earth or up among the stars.

I live in a house that has a howl, and it is there for me: something I could not buy or build or imagine. But I assume I have earned it. I have no further plans or questions.

Tourist Baiting

With all due respect, the tourist I encountered at the roadside park near our home had just driven through a hillbilly mini-mall called "Booger Hollow"—a tourist trap a few miles to the south on Scenic Byway Seven. He would understandably have questions.

Also, I was sitting there at a park table, clad in bib overalls, and alas! I was whittling. I was working on a cedar walking stick that I fully intended to use on forays down into the woods. It was a pit stop for me, on a walk I was taking while Wifey was off at a club meeting. I was not smoking a corncob pipe, and my teeth were all there, but I suppose I looked like the brochure hillbilly this guy was expecting to see. He sidled over to me.

"So," he said, "you from around here?"

And I said, "Yep," and kept on whittling. All right, I was baiting him. I am bad, okay?

"Ah. Great view." I'd say he was about fifty; well dressed guy, too. Innocent.

"Yep." Absolutely preoccupied. I scratched a little at about this part.

"Well, uh, I see you're carving something there."

"Yep. Walkin' stick. Cedar."

"That the best kind?"

"Yep. Tough and purty." I whittled some more.

"So. Looks like all the leaves are about down. Winter's on the way."

"Yep. Happens fast." I blew away some chips, took a sighting, closed one eye.

"Thanksgiving's coming up soon."

"Yep. Next week." I actually spat at this point—quite accurately, too. I actually spat.

"My favorite holiday. I always say we should be thankful."

"Yep. Thankful." I spat again. I don't know, I just thought it fit in.

Then he hit me with something I could work with. "So, what do they do for Thanksgiving—around here?" he said, gazing at The View.

Back when I was teaching high school English I used to have the kids set up a whole culture, complete with traditions and holidays of their invention, as a communications project: emerging leadership, role playing, all that group activity crap. I remembered strange holidays we came up with. I was ready.

"Well," I said thoughtfully, "first we boil up a batch of hog jowls and possum belly, all a-floatin' in a mess of collard greens and black-eyed peas. Then we strip all the kids and paint 'em purple with mulberry juice and then pack 'em in egg crates with Styrofoam peanuts! The adults shave their heads and hop around on one foot, in tight circles, a-moanin' and a-groanin'— with banjo pickin' in the background. At noon, we kill us a nanny goat, decorate the toilet with wax and feathers, make love to our first cousins, and bury Granny Jones in the back yard. What do you do at your house?"

"Turkey and dressing," he said wearily, slowly nodding his head and looking down. "Sweet potatoes and marshmallow, cranberry sauce—like that. Pumpkin pie." It was about over, I could tell. He'd "made" me.

"Strange. Smacks of something just mildly pagan," I said, letting him see that I had teeth.

He was one of those people who can raise one eyebrow at a time, and he did, and I broke up.

"Why do I get the feeling I am being led down the garden path here?" he said.

"I haven't the foggiest. Our gardens are a joke, and we

haven't got room for a path. Where was it you said you were from?"

"Cleveland. What about you? Really."

"Houston," I said. Then I apologized for my arrogance and filled him in on what Wifey and I were up to. We laughed a little, and I invited him over to the house for a look at our view.

But, you know, that guy never showed up. Go figure. You try to be neighborly...

The Cookie Mess

Right after "peak color" in late October and early November, the tour buses packed with gray Americans would disappear from Scenic Byway Seven, the Cliff House restaurant would close its doors, Branson traffic would find its way around the mountains, the clouds would move in close, and we would have the high ground to ourselves. The fog would freeze, and the resulting "winter wonderland" effect would be for our eyes only. Ah, exclusivity at last.

Everybody needs to experience a little exclusivity before he dies. It's when you get to see something that the tourists don't. Mere mortals are denied these wonders. In our part of the hills, the people who pay for the pleasure by putting up with the ice storms get to see beauty beyond description. Wifey and I learned to expect dazzling, glitzy ice, rather than warm, Currier and Ives snow. The trees turned to crystal and came smashing down on the electrical lines, "plunging us into darkness," and all that. We learned the tricks of survival, like all the locals, and we liked the place.

I attached a great deal of macho nonsense to this life. Somehow, we were tougher than others—somewhat smug about having a little extra ice, a little more wind, yada yada yada. Sometimes we got a bit more moisture than Mt. Sherman or Mt. Judea, our winds were stronger, and we were just tougher than "flatlanders." I could argue that we needed to be cut some slack because we were being put upon by The Elements! But nobody listens to me.

One thing I was fairly certain of, though, was that the electrical power company did not have any particular axe to grind with me. It seemed to me that if they could have the lines open and could sell me electricity, they would go with that! I thought the crews were heroic, working all night in the cold to plug us all back into the world. To the neighbor lady, it was all political, and some were getting power (because they knew somebody) while others were being deliberately ignored: placed at risk, being allowed to freeze in the dark.

"Oh, you can scoff at me all you want, but mark my words..." she would chant, and then there would be "shocking" tales of woe , "current" events, "juicy" gossip.

The cookie mess occurred right in the middle of one of our best ice storm/power failures. We had made it to another December, and Christmas was impending: coming over our exposed and unprepared household like a ground blizzard—totally unexpected, as usual. I was terrified, because it was illegal for me to buy Wifey food, clothing, shelter, jewelry, cosmetics, personal pampering services, candy, flowers, publications, or booze—without her personal pre-approval. A good Christmas present might be a promise to remove a nearby mountain or instantly replace a swatch of clear-cutting next door. I, on the other hand, was easy: I didn't want anything, could not think of anything that I wanted or needed.

The latest ice storm had shut us in together with those thoughts in our collective craw. Naturally, we hiked over to the neighbor lady's place to say hello and to look at someone else. It was a nice crisp day, beautiful to the point of the ridiculous.

"I don't care how many lines are down," the neighbor lady was telling the light company on the phone as she waved us in, "I am a poor old woman, and I am starving and freezing in the dark. If you can light up the Wainwrights and the Vandergrifts, you can damn sure light me up!" And she slammed down the phone.

"Howdy," said Wifey. "Just thought we'd drop by and say hello. How ya' doin'?"

"Oh, I'm fine. I've got phone, gas heat, battery TV, lots of canned goods, like everybody else. Only thing is, I can't bake my cookies! And the sale is Friday!"

I had heard all about the sale. In early December, down in the village, the whole community had a chance to drop by The Senior Citizens Center and buy gallons of home-made cookies and candies. These goodies were created and donated by the same people who ended up buying them, of course, and the proceeds went toward toys and coats for needy families. It was yet another conspiracy to put money into the right place and help the unfortunate, and it was a very big deal. "I can't bake mine, either," said Wifey. "I was gonna try some oatmeal/raisin/butterscotch. But our oven is electric, like yours."

Preparing the ultimate cookie was a challenge, an art, a science, a craft, and a matter of pride. There were some in the hills who called Pride a sin, and there were some who called it salvation—the thing that kept one from the abyss! At the county fair, you tried to show the best calf or pig or tomato; at this Christmas cookie set-to, you brought in your best cookies. That kind of pride.

The way the sale worked was simple: you walked into the Center, bought yourself a decorated gallon can, put on a pair of plastic gloves, then went through a gauntlet of yummy, colorful displays, shopping and selecting a full gallon of what you considered the best cookies. You packed your can full, and you went home rich! Simplicity itself.

However, there were other rules. The cookies were being monitored by Watchers, and the first ones to sell out were automatically considered the best ones. There was no blue ribbon, nobody got "The Crystal Cookie" trophy, and there was no feature article in the local paper; still, everybody but EVERYBODY knew whose cookies went first. It was a matter of bragging rights. The neighbor lady was always in the middle of the fray. It was war.

"I want to go with my chocolate cocoanut macaroons this year," she said to Wifey. "I tried that other thing last year—forget what it was. But it came in second. This year, I'm going for their throats!"

"Who won last year?" I asked innocently. Stupid. We were sitting at the table by that time, sipping hot cocoa, and Wifey kicked me so hard under that table that I thought my leg would be hanging there by a ribbon of skin! Simple little question.

"Ma Wainwright, that's who!" snarled the neighbor lady. "She cobbled up some fool concoction that looked good and tasted like cardboard, and those idiots cleaned her out in three minutes. I still think she hired it done."

"How would she do that?" I asked. Wifey had her shoes off, but that one hurt, too. And she was right to do it. I understand that now.

"She hired someone to buy her cookies first—I'd stake my life on it. Mine sold right away, but then I was honest. I just put my cookies out there and let the customer decide." A smug sneer.

"Well, how many cookies are we talkin' about here?" I quizzed.

"Six dozen! If they would plug in my electricity, I would show you some cookies! I'll bet the Wainwrights have got power, and I know for a fact that the Vandergrifts have got it because I saw their lights last night over the mountains to the South. Some people get electricity and some don't." She seemed just a little bitter.

I had met Ma Wainwright at an auction, and I knew who she was from a time when we moved Double Dog Darrell's piano out of her parlor. I only knew that she was a character and that she liked to dress in bright yellow fleece outfits.

"She looks like one of those Caterpillar bulldozers," said the neighbor lady. "She probably eats a dozen cookies for every dozen she contributes."

"Doesn't everybody?" said Wifey. I kicked her under the table—just a little. I had my shoes off, too. Fair is fair.

"She looks like a big yellow barn. I'll bet she's seven axe-handles across the hind end. And that yellow makes her look all the bigger—like a Three Mile Island canary!"

"Well, she's colorful," I said. "No pun intended."

"The electric company plugs in the rich people first, and

they let the rest of us sit in the dark. And this year I don't get to bake my cookies at all, and the Wainwrights and the Vandergrifts of the world do! The system is rotten to the core."

Well, I mumbled the obvious — low, to myself, mind you: I did not blurt it out.

"What did you say?' the neighbor lady challenged.

"Nothing. I was just babbling."

"I heard you. And I don't think it's funny. You're new on this hill, and you don't know everything. This power thing is all political. They light up who they feel like lighting up. If they don't like you or if you don't have influence, you can sit in the dark for a week That is how the cookie crumbles, Mr. Smarty Pants."

"But..."

"Shut up," said Wifey.

"Yes, dear."

Well, they had me outnumbered. Wifey had me outnumbered all by herself. So did the neighbor lady — all by herself. And I did shut up. It was uncomfortable for a moment, but then the phone rang.

"Hello? Yes, I'm still dark here. Who is this?" The neighbor lady's eyes got big, and I knew she had been torpedoed pretty good. Gritting her teeth, she became uncharacteristically polite. "Well, thank you, Thelma, but I am going to hold out for some electricity. But thank you anyway, and I'll keep that in mind. Look, I can't talk now — I've got company. But thank you. I'll probably see you at the Center. Good-bye." She slammed the phone down hard, picked it up and slammed it down again, and repeated the procedure once more. I swear, steam came out of her ears!

"So, who's Thelma?" I asked innocently. I think my left kneecap is going to need some tightening. Wifey let me have it good. I swear, you try to have a little conversation...

"That was Thelma Wainwright," rasped the neighbor lady. "She wants to offer me her oven! Her electricity is on! She wants me to bake my cookies at her place! Can you imagine that? She's got the knife into me, and she's gonna twist! She's gonna split me open like an overly ripe melon! She's gonna dump my guts right out on the ground! Of all the low-down, scheming, nasty, rotten, scummy things to do..."

"Oh, she means well," said Wifey. "Probably just wants to help."

"You don't get it, do you? She's over there mocking me! She has the power to get the power..." and she started to get a little befuddled. "She...she..that..that overgrown, pus yellow blimp! That..that nasty, rotten...";!

The phone rang again.

"Hello! Oh, hello, Thelma. Really? No kidding? Well, if that's the way they do it, who are we, right? Yes. Well, thank you. See you later." And she slammed the phone down again.

"Whaaat?" I ventured.

"I don't believe it. I just absolutely do not believe it. If I live to be a hundred and five, I will never understand these dirty, putrid people." (The neighbor lady did not consider herself a "local" because she had moved to the ridge a mere dozen or so years ago. "These people" were the natives!)

Wifey didn't say anything, and I held my breath. The neighbor lady cooled to a fast simmer, and that was good, because boiling was about to bring on a stroke.

"Ma Wainwright says that they're going to turn off her electricity now so that they can plug in our part of the line! She says the light company called her and told her to expect an interruption of service while it's being done. Probably so that she won't have uneven baking on her cookies! The jaundiced bitch!" The neighbor lady delivered the line with such sarcasm, such bitterness, such rage that I was deeply moved.

"Well, if you get plugged in, we should get plugged in, too," said Wifey hopefully. "It's the same line, isn't it?"

"Yeah," she said, fanning herself. "But Thelma Wainwright has to sacrifice so that we can have electricity. There can't really be a God, can there?"

I understood. Even if the neighbor lady's cookies sold out first, Ma Wainwright would be able to take some of the credit. At least, I knew that was what the neighbor lady was sweating.

"And we'll all get to bake our cookies, right?—all of us," chirped Wifey.

"Yeah."

"And all of us," I said, "will take part in this wonderful act of Christian charity. The kids will have their toys, their little coats." Then a disgraceful thought hit me, and I blurted it out. "I don't know: has anybody ever thought of just collecting a bunch of money instead of going to all the trouble with the cookie baking?"

"Bite your tongue," said the neighbor lady. "What would be the fun in that?"

✀

She was right, of course. The whole cookie mess was a custom and a social occasion. It was a gig. And in our part of the hills, that was important. We bought two gallons.

Cold Cedar

It was an epic ice storm. Down around Little Rock the young pines along the highways were bowed down or snapped off. The valley, all the way to Fort Smith, even places south of there, and especially our mountains to the North—and well up into Missouri—were an official disaster area. The power was off, the phones were out, and the back roads were impassable and impossible. And it was all so spectacularly beautiful, so crystal crested and diamond decked, so frost frilled and glass glowing, that I was wandering around with my little Nikon recording masterpieces at every turn. And writing bad poetry.

Then Old Hubert showed up with his home-made ice shoes. He'd made it all the way from his house, within sight of our northern windows, but a very slippery quarter of a mile that day. We were "rim folk," I had decided: people who lived on top of the precarious rim of what people were calling The Grand Canyon of the Ozarks. (Engelval, to German settlers; Big Creek to the others.) Old Hubert was a Chicago boy. He was tough. We were neighbors, especially in times of diversity and cabin fever. (Just old goats, really: baggy overalls, drippy noses, a little lost.)

"My dog fell out of the yard," Old Hubert said for openers.

"I hate it when that happens," I replied without blinking. I was chiseling three inches of ice out of my driveway with a big steel bar.

"I mean it! She got too close to the brink, and she skidded down there to the first shelf. Almost went over the cliff."

Our yards were jokes, really: treacherous places. There was

little level land on Old Hubert's place or ours, and in summer, mowing grass was a challenge and a thrill, sometimes impossible. Even small errors could be painful. In winter we stayed away from the brink, and in ice storms we stayed indoors. But you can't communicate that to a dog.

"She's down there on that ledge. I saw her get close to the edge, and I yelled at her, but she lost it and went howling down the slope. Dug in just shy of the cliff. Old Jake and me roped up the Vandergrift kid and lowered him to her, but he couldn't tie her up." Yeah, Old Jake, Old Hubert, Old Me.

"Dog's probably scared to death."

"Yeah. And cold. Happened yesterday. She was down there all night. You mighta heard her." It was not an accusation.

"Naw. We stayed inside by the battery powered TV and the gas fireplace last night. Didn't stick my nose outside."

"I heard the cattle are fallin' down in the pastures—doin' the splits! Can't get up—and folks can't get 'em up—not with three solid inches of clear, blue ice on everything."

We had heard the stories, too. Thousands were in the dark, getting cold, shut off from everybody, in trouble. Up where we were, people had back-up systems for most exigencies.

"You pull the Vandergrift kid up out of there okay?" I was wondering. Old Jake, another neighbor, was a physical wreck: ran around with oxygen bottles and inhalers and a cane! But he had helped.

"Yeah—but without the dog. I'd go down there myself, but I'm too damned old."

"Man, there's a lot of that going around," I said. "I fell on my kadooky right where you're standing, just this morning. I'm sore already. About busted my butt."

"Get some old sneakers and put some screws in them—or get some golf shoes goin' for you. Or do this," Old Hubert said, showing me his invention. He had cut footprints out of quarter-inch plywood and run several screws through them and duct taped them to his boots. He could walk around, the points of the screws digging into the blue ice. Mobility!

"That'll work," I said. But he already knew that. What he

wanted to hear was some new thinking on how to get that dog off that ledge. I needed more coaxing—a real pity/guilt trip.

"Wish I could get some of these onto that dog's feet. She climbed part-way up, poor old thing, right on the ice, but then she skidded back down, looked over the edge—another 30 foot drop—and then just quit. There's some blood. Got any ideas?"

"I'd have to see it," I told him. "Let's make me some ice shoes."

I had to help, of course. It would hardly be neighborly to tell fellow rim folk to handle their own problems. No way I was going down there on a rope, though, to tangle with that dog; but I thought there might be another way, if we could look things over and strategize and re-think the situation. Then there was the other aspect: how often do you get in on an adventure that starts with a dog falling out of a yard?

In the garage, Old Hubert and I put together the ultimate ice shoes for my purposes: sneakers with hex-nuts and extra insoles. I tried them out in the driveway, and it was a victory. I could go.

I had to explain to Wifey that I was going over to the neighbor's house to try to retrieve a dog that had fallen out of his backyard. That should have stunned her a little.

"Oh," she said, and went on with her coupon clipping. A dog lover, too! I supposed that the weird events of the past couple of days had jaded her. We had wondered and speculated the previous evening about the animals in the forest, the birds, the trees. How would they fare?—the deer, the turkeys, the foxes? I guess she was just prepared, somehow. I never understood her. But she had been a nurse for many years, and I guess she was simply ready.

Old Hubert and I picked our way over to his place and around back of the house. We approached the stranded animal from the point of entry. There were scratches in the ice, and skid marks where the kid had been lowered by rope. I could see where they had tied off the top of the rope, and the whole story of the attempted rescue was there in the shattered wreckage of the icy slope. It was not hard to see why the boy had failed to secure the dog: the ledge below was narrow, and the drop beyond the brink was formidable. The dog was old and terrified.

But now the dog was gone. I had prepared myself for a pathetic, frustrated, shivering hound, all worn out and ready for me to help her, somehow. All the way over to Old Hubert's place, I had imagined the SPCA Medal of Bravery being placed around my neck at a ceremony in Little Rock! I thought of the grateful animal, whimpering and licking my face! I thought how pleased Wifey would be. And proud.

But the dog was gone. There was some pinkish ice down there, but no dog.

"Cedar!" Old Hubert yelled, and he whistled. "Cedar! Where are you, girl?" he whistled again. Nothing. "God. Hope she didn't drop over the ledge," he said.

"She's probably found another way up," I said. "Dogs are good at stuff like that..." My voice trailed off to nothing. Old Hubert wasn't buying it.

"Cedar!" he shouted. He had a good loud whistle, too—the kind I could never produce, no matter how much I blew on my fingers. "Cedar!" And another shrill whistle.

Far off into the canyon, there was a clear yip! I swear it. Trouble was, Old Hubert couldn't hear it at all, and I could barely hear it myself.

"Cedar!"

"Wait. Shhhh! I think I heard a dog."

We waited and listened hard. And the little yip came again! Old Hubert whistled, and the yipping became frenetic!

"She's out that way, Hubert. I heard her! She's working her way around the shelf! Maybe she'll find a way up."

"I don't hear nothin'."

"Whistle again."

Old Hubert split a fingernail on the next blast, I'm sure. And, way back along the shelf, which ran two or three miles along the side of the mountain, I was sure a dog barked— excitedly! But the barking seemed more distant. I started thinking the dog was smart. We looked at the lay of the land once again, and, with all the ice, straight home was not the way for the dog. The answer for Cedar lay somewhere else, perhaps down the ridge somewhere.

We both yelled for a while, but soon other dogs in other directions chimed in. Cedar's voice faded and was gone. Then our voices faded, too. For a while there, Old Hubert thought he heard dogs barking, but he was not certain.

"Forecast says it'll be in the teens tonight," he said, and he gave me a grave look.

For a while, I said nothing, but I did some thinking. "We can't go where she's gone, even with our fancy ice grippers. And we'd never catch up."

∿

We turned away from the abyss, trying to imagine the next move. Maybe she would find a way down, and hook up with some valley folks and find her way home later. Maybe she could find shelter in a cave or at some old abandoned cabin. There were enough of both on the mountain. Certainly every exposed surface, down to the smallest twig, was encased in ice. The canopy was a billion prisms, and the floor of the forest was covered with fragments of ice and icy twigs shaken down from above by the wind—ankle deep in some places, as if a chemist's lab had exploded, or "all the windows of Heaven" had shattered. All of that on top of three inches of sheet ice.

"Wind is good," Old Hubert rationalized. "It's gotta bring better weather. In a day or so, it'll warm up. But tonight, I don't know."

"She'll be okay." I could not believe that I was being the "up" person. Usually, I could recite a dozen flavors of doom at a moment's notice. "Cedar's a smart dog. She'll figure it out."

We thought of everything: no way to catch the dog; clearly up to the animal herself; even a rescue squad or a helicopter would scare her to death; no such thing as a tractor beam; no way to lock on her coordinates and beam her aboard; worm holes out of the question; yada yada yada. Finally, Old Hubert looked at me and said, "Well?"

"Well what?"

"It's time for us to snatch victory from the jaws of defeat, right?"

"Yeah."

"When the goin' gets tough, the tough get goin', right?"

"Yeah."

"Well?"

"Well, what?"

"What are we gonna do? It's a sad thing. She's in the slipperiest place ever was, and she's stuck!"

❧

So, as usual, it was time to do something stupid. We decided to go after the dog. We chose a promising place where there seemed to be some footing and lots of trees around to prevent long skids and to break falls. We checked the ground carefully. We reasoned that we could work our way toward the sound of Cedar's last yip, using the forest itself as a...never mind. It was grievously flawed thinking.

We stepped carefully into the thicket, watching our feet carefully so as to make as few mistakes as possible. We were about twenty feet into the woods when a gust of cold, whipping wind hit the neighborhood: not a friendly zephyr or a harbinger of better things, either! This was a stiff, sudden blast. And Old Hubert and I were in a hard hat area to trump all hard hat areas! Overhead, the branches crashed together, and everything broke loose and dropped, knocking more and more debris loose as it dropped. We were suddenly being strafed by jagged, sharp, heavy ice missiles: crystal shrapnel, stinging and thick!

Well, we had our overalls on, of course, and heavy jackets. But not helmets. I saw the chunk that whacked Old Hubert on the nose, just before my glasses were knocked off. I trampled the glasses underfoot clamoring for clear ground. And Old Hubert bled. For two old coots, we moved fast.

"Damn!" said Old Hubert as we reached safety. "I won't be doin' that again."

"But we had to try," I said nobly.

"But we're not nuts, right?"

He really wanted to know. Another blast of cold wind hit us there, but we were on the road by then. All through the woods a clattering uproar, punctuated by occasional cracks as larger limbs snapped off, echoed and menaced. I manufactured some eyewear, bending the carcass of my twisted and flattened glasses into a familiar shape, and I looked deep into the forest. White spears stabbed down and exploded into glassy fragments where we had fumbled about a few moments earlier—and all down through the beautiful trees, a chaotic storm of splinters.

"I'm goin home," said Old Hubert. "Gonna sit by the stove with my wife and have some coffee."

"Better put a Band Aid on your beak, too, Hubert."

He took off his glove and tapped the skinned spot on the bridge of his nose. Blood.

"Damn. I'm wounded."

"Yeah. Get under your roof. I'll go home and sit with Wifey and look out the window. I've had enough fresh air for one day."

"Yeah."

"Dog'll be okay. She's smart."

❧

I went toward my place and Old Hubert went toward his. At our age, a hip fracture would about do us in, so we both took it slow and easy, carefully placing each step, staying away from the brink. All the poetry had gone out of the day. I was reminded of jungle photography: visually, the picture is stunningly beautiful, but you just know something is gnawing at the photographer's leg, or wrapping around it! The beautiful ice was just not safe. I crept, I'm sad to say, into my driveway, along the frozen retaining wall, and around to the sheltered back door of our warm home. Sanctuary. Heroism over. Period.

❧

Of course, Cedar was lying there in front of the gas log

fireplace when I came stumbling into the house. Wifey the Old Nurse had some cotton and a bottle and was daubing Cedar's paws, and Cedar was stretched out, dry and warm, and smiling. Her red coat was glowing in the firelight. I just shook my head.

I made a move for the telephone, hesitated because I knew it was dead, and caught my glasses as they tried to crash to the tile floor and smash like so much ice. They were fogged anyway.

"Phone works," said Wifey. "I called Edna half an hour ago. Dog's fine. Came here and scratched at the door while you two old fools were yelling out there in the woods."

I know that dog was smiling.

Barter

The disappearance of the neighbor lady had nothing to do with barter, I say. Others say that it was the obligation game that grew out of the bartering that did her in. I liked her, and that's a fact: she was feisty, cantankerous even! And often she was just plain misinformed, prejudiced, and silly. But she was never old, although she was chronologically older than Wifey and I. I miss her (and especially her brownies), but she is definitely gone.

If she were here theorizing about her departure herself, she might say it had something to do with The Bottomless Pit. That would have made it colorful. She loved that bottomless pit, and she never got to show it to me. It served as a catch-all for everything unexplained or otherwise mysterious in her life on the ridge. She would certainly have blamed The Bottomless Pit (at least figuratively) for her disappearance, if she had not been personally involved and fully informed. She chose to disappear, after all.

❦

The ancient concept of bartering is alive in the hinterlands of America. Notice I did not say "alive and well." Because bartering, like any form of trade, can get way out of hand!

Wifey turned out to be good at it. She got involved with locals by trading a few cookies for a little extra help with moving in; she escalated by doing a little light nursing (off the books and under the table) in exchange for some cucumbers; then she traded me off for a sack of apples. (I had to dig a hole.) We raked leaves for somebody and took the leaves home to our compost heap as payment. Goods for services, vegetables for fruits, canned goods for raw materials, bread for broccoli, firewood for manure, a wood stove for roof repair, almost anything for peanut butter: Wifey did cut some deals. One of her best was when she paid a lady for taking one of our kittens off our hands by offering me to pluck 200 bag worms off the shrubbery down at the courthouse.   How could that ever go wrong? Everybody seems to profit in a barter—except the IRS—and that should make it a good thing! Each party seems to get what he wants, and there is a great deal of sociability involved. One of our deals (four feet of countertop for a toaster oven, I believe), lasted until well after dark: not because of the trade itself but because of the clinging to the door, the slow amble to the car, the long and reluctant good-bye between the couple in the car and Wifey and me (hanging onto the door handles and dragging along the driveway, and the standing in the middle of Highway Seven and waving at the disappearing taillights, yelling, "We have ice cream!"). A good barter can end a lonesome spell.

But then there is the game of obligation that can evolve from such a practice. And that is how, according to some people, the neighbor lady ultimately disappeared from the ridge.

Wifey brought a small plastic container of chili-mac over to the neighbor lady—just "out of the clear blue sky"—one sunny winter day. "Pop this in your micro later, and you've got dinner."

"Why, thank you. I was going to have to come up with something. It's not easy cooking for one, you know. I hate to bother."

Yeah. Widow. Her husband had been gone for a while, and we never knew him. But we found her and liked her, and she was, after all, our neighbor. We developed drop-in privileges, and the ugliness began.

The neighbor lady felt obligated by that dollop of chili-mac, and she paid us back. She invited us over for a little casserole dinner that very week, and it was good. Then *we* were obligated. A whole dinner for one splotch of chili-mac? Wifey hit her with some cookies right away, and she volleyed back with fudge! That quick! In just a couple of exchanges, we were all the way up to fudge: decadent fudge, too—nuts and the whole bit.

Before long I was climbing on her roof and she was coming up with roast beef; I pounded a few nails, and she hit me with a bunch of her husband's books; Wifey helped her with her curtains and she tinted Wifey's hair. Once I tried but failed to help out with an electrical problem, and she hit me with rhubarb/strawberry upside-down cake anyway..

But who was keeping score, right? Everyone was keeping score, especially the neighbor lady! "I don't know what I'll ever do to repay you..." she would say. "Forget it: we're neighbors," we would say. But secretly we were keeping score, too. "After we do this, she will owe us. Maybe she will make some more fudge." Petty stuff like that.

"Let my husband cut that limb off for you. It could fall on your car," Wifey said hopefully.

"He could break his neck doing that. It's up there pretty good."

"So, what's the downside here?" Wifey always had a dry sense of humor.

"I'll make my brownies," said the neighbor lady. It was a threat.

❧

The brownies forever obligated both of us to the neighbor lady. Even though it was I who climbed up with my manly chain saw and lopped off the limb, Wifey got to participate in the payoff. (She did hold the ladder.) The Brownies were chocolaty and nutty, they had frosting, and they were a little crispy (the way I like them), and they had scoops of ice cream on them, and it just wasn't fair. And although I tried to hide how really deeply moving the whole experience was, I had to say, "Please allow me to forfeit my immortal soul..." or some such tearful utterance as I hugged the neighbor lady and groveled at her feet. Wifey was subdued: appreciative, but a little distressed, too. At table, she kicked chips out of my shins to calm me down.

"How will we ever pay her back for those brownies?" she said at home.

"How will we ever earn more of them?—that is the question!"

"You really did sort of tip your hand, you know, foaming at the mouth like that. They weren't that good."

"Yes they were."

Wifey paused a moment, but then admitted it. "You're right. We're doomed."

❧

Eventually, after several exchanges in which I would say or do, invent or manufacture, steal or kidnap, hustle or rustle just about anything for a brownie score with the neighbor lady, Mother Nature Herself stepped in.

❧

It was a dark and stormy night again: dark and stormy like it gets up on top. A cold, whipping wind, freezing rain, and a plumbing problem down under the neighbor lady's double-wide! It was delicious.

The neighbor lady could show me where the problem was, and I could see what had to be done, but it was a foul night for man or beast, and I had her by the throat! I could smell those brownies, taste them, feel them in my soul. I was going to get so messed up, expose myself to the elements in such an extreme manner, and contribute such a priceless service that mere human brownies would never suffice! I crawled through the cold mud, getting "soaked to the skin" in the process; I lay on my back under there while Wifey trained a flashlight on the ailing valve; I grunted loudly and even bled a little. Ice water flew everywhere. It took a long time—a long, long time. I suffered—rent my garments—exerted greatly. When I was through, there were not enough brownies in the hills to pay me back. I emerged looking like I had been trapped in a coal mine for several days. And Wifey was wet and bedraggled, too, and a little hoarse from shouting helpful advice. Just to make things worse, the repair worked!

It was fully a year after that when scuttlebutt hit the mountain web that our neighbor was moving away: fully a year, I insist. We were sad to hear it. She had relatives elsewhere, that's all, and it was lonely on the mountain, in spite of her network of friends. That is what it was—not the barter thing. I had brownies and fudge and casseroles enough. Wifey, too. I don't care what they say, we were off the hook by the time the neighbor lady sold out and moved away. Her son. She wanted to be near her son, in a warmer climate! It took months and months to get it all together, and we helped her with that as much as she would let us. But she wouldn't let us help much.

One day it was over and she was gone, that's all. The game of obligation was harmless—just fun: it rose out of affection and neighborliness and compassion—maybe a little friendly greed and some flattery, but that was just custom, tradition. Really. It did not cause her to go away. I insist.

Besides, in the end, just before her son drove her away, the neighbor lady handed me a large Tupperware container just stuffed with those brownies. And then they skipped town! The way I figure it, she's ahead now. But, really, who's keeping score?

Double-Dog Darrell and The Bottomless Pit

On any brightly moonlit night, there would be a tug-of-war in our living room as I was torn between TV and the magnificent view outside the window, between comfortable monotony and true stimulation, between the doldrums of safety and the feeling that something awesome could happen any minute.

The wild housecats on the upper deck of our disappointing house suddenly focused on something in the front yard—four of them, arching their backs one-by-one as they snapped to what was happening, then moving close to the sliding glass door and closer to each other. I tore myself away from the TV and checked it out. Shadows. Wolves. Horses. Double-Dog Darrell. This time I was warned.

It was December, and there was a full moon. My random splash of Christmas lights out front beat back the shadows on that side of the house, but The View (out back) was all silver-plated by intense moonlight. Ho hum, more grandeur!—miles of it, almost painfully beautiful. We had the TV on anyway, but I was drifting back and forth, selfishly trying to absorb all of it.

I was ready for it when the knock came. There was no prelude of thumping and stomping as our visitor came up the wooden steps onto the front porch. This was Double-Dog Darrell, and it was a soundless approach. I had never before been warned of his arrival . I felt secure, somehow. I opened the door promptly, thinking peanut butter all the way. There would be peanut butter now: there always was when Darrell and I were getting along.

"Get your pants on," he said without any hello. "You're

going for a horseback ride." He held out two jars of smooth. (The government was not handing out crunchy at the time.) The peanut butter meant that Double-Dog was in good shape: friendly, healthy, sociable, straight.

"Come on in, Darrell. Warm yourself by the TV. And thank you!" I accepted the peace offering and got him inside. He looked bigger and darker indoors, and wilder. He was dressed for the trail and the cold, never mind about the color.

Wifey and Double-Dog had buried the hatchet during the year sometime—I forget just when—and they could be in a room together now, in sort of a cease-fire mode. She had thrown him out after their set-to the previous year, but now things were quiet. My own feud with him had been short-lived, unsatisfying, and totally understandable. You praise poetry, you don't criticize it. Although I found Darrell's poetry flawed, I should have kept quiet, approved heartily, and gone on with life. I was guilty of poetry myself, and I knew better.

But all of that was behind us that night. Wifey was warm, I was infused with moonlight, and Double-Dog Darrell was medicated. I was sure I could adjust things, no matter what the scheme.

"We don't have a lot of time," said Darrell. "The moon'll go down, and there'll be about an hour and a half of darkness just before sun-up. For now, we've got light. Get your pants on." He was grinning and looking me in the eye, probing.

"I've got pants on. I don't do horseback rides. It's nighttime. It's not really warm outside. I am perfectly comfortable right here. What the hell are you talking about?"

"You'll need jeans over those sweat pants. You'll ride a horse tonight—out in the cold. You keep saying you're a Minnesota boy and cold don't bother you. 'Put up or shut up' time has arrived. You've been comfortable in here by the TV too long. So, put away the peanut butter, and get your pants on. Oh, and what the hell I'm talkin' about here is The Bottomless Pit." I froze. (And it was not the only time I froze that night.) "The Bottomless Pit?"

"You've heard about it; God knows you've talked about

it enough, and asked about it and made fun of it and obsessed over it. Now you're gonna see it—at about midnight, after half a horseback ride." He had his glasses off because they were fogged. He was pinkish and drippy, mopping his nose with a red bandana, and flashing his challenging grin at me, glancing at Wifey.

Wifey! Well, I knew she would not allow this. I couldn't even get away from her to do a little Christmas shopping. No way she would let me out of her sight overnight. Wifey would save me. I turned to her in desperation and gave her my most helpful look.

But I could see "the future in the instant." (A little *Macbeth* there.) I have moments like that, when I'm about to slip over the brink: intuitive moments when I know what is coming next. I knew that, unless I did something decisive and effective, instantly, I was doomed. "Wifey?" I said pitifully.

"A ride in the moonlight! On a horsey! Out in the cold! Getting to the bottom of the old Bottomless Pit story that you're so fond of. It'll be good for you," said my wife, my refuge, my partner in life, my healer, my rescuer.

"But..." I argued passionately.

"You never go anywhere with your friends. You don't socialize. You *have* no friends! You claim you can't get away—that I confine you. But you love the cold, and you're a Minnesota boy..."

"But..."

"I've heard you say so a hundred times. And you throw in little remarks about the locals and their Bottomless Pit fantasy all the time. It's to the point where you're the only one who talks about it. Bottomless Pit this, Bottomless Pit that. Now you can go there. So, go for it! You've got the night off! Sounds like a plan to me."

"Get your pants on."

"Keep your shirt on! Look, horses hate me. In broad daylight, horses hate me. Twenty-five pounds ago they hated me! Twenty-five years ago they hated me."

"It'll be good for you to get out—do some real male

bonding—have a little fun," said Wifey, throwing a pair of blue jeans at me. "Get your pants on."

"But..."

"And, here," she said, handing me a sack from the fridge, "I've made up a few sandwiches—with mustard! See you tomorrow."

Now I went numb. (And it was not the last time I went numb that night.) I was at a temporary loss for words. I scrolled through betrayal, conspiracy, covert activity, disloyalty, deceit, vengefulness, guile, double-dealing, duplicity, meanness, and "throwing me to the wolves" as I stood there in my warm, satisfactory house, with my pants in my hand. They had evidently met at the Senior Citizens Center in town and planned the whole thing—all of them, maybe: the gray geezers, the pool players, the guilty quilt hookers, the tightly-knit knitters, the crafty cooks—the whole mob, and Double-Dog Darrell and my wife! I was toast. Cold toast this time.

ॐ

"I thought you didn't like to be alone on the mountain at night," I said to Wifey, desperately, but without the trace of a whine.

"Quit whining," she said, "and get your pants on. I'll be fine."

"But..."

"You've got to grab all the gusto," Darrell said, grinning.

"YOU'VE got to grab all the gusto," I stated, rather boldly for me. "Me? I've got to zap a little popcorn in the micro and hunker down over 'Law and Order'..."

"You hate 'Law and Order,'" said Wifey. "Get your butt on the horse and scram!"

"You did that last night and the night before. Get movin'!" Darrell was physically pushing me now, and Wifey was pulling.

I stopped both of them right there: stood them back from me, disengaged the touching routine, period. (I allow just so much, and no more, after all. You can push me just so far, and then I bow my neck and I make my move.) (I have a lot of my mother in me.)

"Okay," I said, "Let's do it!"

&

"See there," Wifey said immediately to her friend Double-Dog Darrell, "I told you so. You're about to pull an all-nighter."

Yeah, that's right. They snookered me. I was downhill of an avalanche of conspiracy; I could see that! I growled and griped my way through my closet, furiously clawing together some boots and some warm layers of insulation, a gun, some gloves, heavy socks, and a flashlight. I heard voices—real merriment in the kitchen—as I dug around in the chaos. "All right, you scummy cruds, let's go," I snarled. "You work for years to get the damned place tight and weather-proof and warm, and then you've gotta go out there with friggin' Trigger and freeze your ass off in the moonlight because some raving madman has made up with your wife..." (The closet muffled all of that, and a lot more. Usually I had to go out into the woods, far away from Wifey, to tell her off. I discovered that night that the closet was good for grousing. A coup.)

When I emerged with my gear, there were three people waiting around the table by the big window on the View side: Darrell, Wifey, and Madge Colstad, Wifey's club buddy and auction companion.

"Well, Hi," I said to Madge. "What brings you to our mountain tonight?"

"Your dear wife does not want to be alone here at night. I don't blame her." She was obviously there by appointment. This had been in the works for a long time.

"Right. Looks like everything is pretty well set, then." I could have said a lot of things at that point. Afterwards, on the trail, I thought of terrible things I could have said: just brilliant, scathing volleys of insult and invective—language I had learned from generations of teenagers during my teaching career—thoughts so base that they made me want to bathe and gargle and spit! But instead, I just let them all know that I was armed, and I said to Double-Dog, "Let's go to the Bottomless Pit!" Dramatic as hell!

Often, after I convince myself that something is impossible, I do it anyway.

"His name isn't Trigger," protested Double-Dog. "It's Hacksaw. He's real gentle, aren't you, Hacksaw?" And he kissed my horse right on the lips! Then he turned to me with the big grin and said, "All you have to do is hold on. He won't go left, he won't go right, he won't go at all unless the horse in front of him does. That's Muffin and me. He will trot if me and Muffin trot; he will gallop if me and Muffin gallop; he will stop when we stop, go when we go, throw you off when I get off. So, when I stop and dismount, you do it at the same time. Got it?"

I looked Hacksaw over by the light of Santa and his sleigh there in the front yard. To me, Hacksaw looked brown, mostly, and big: certainly dark. That's about all I know about horses anyway. "Do I have to kiss him?"

"Not on the lips. You don't know each other that well yet. Right on the forehead, though—on that white blaze. Let him look you over. Pat him gently. Talk to him, and don't say 'Nice horsey' to him. He hates that. You've got a minute to make friends."

Hacksaw was saddled and ready to go. Double-Dog had done some considerable work, and I began to appreciate the effort. A full-scale trail ride was all set up and ready to go. It was evidently important to some people that I make this ride. Maybe this was my Christmas present from someone—or everyone. Maybe people were just sick of hearing about the bottomless pit. I decided to make the best of it for now, survive, and kill them all later. That meant that I would now become this wordless, granite stoic: impervious to pain and cold and terror and fatigue.

I sprung into the saddle during the next five or six minutes. Hacksaw was patient, and he did not bite me as hard as he could have, and I whispered my appreciation, gently pressing my cold pistol against the side of his warm mahogany neck. He seemed to understand me a little—either that or the Christmas lights reflected in his eyes gave him that manic look. I preferred to think we had grown closer suddenly. I was privately terrified anyway.

When Muffin and Darrell headed toward the nativity scene at the little church just down the road, Hacksaw followed, and I hung on. The night was young.

❧

"Think of what is happening here," lectured Double-Dog. "Two men on horseback, accompanied by wolves, are riding in the dead of night out into a wilderness to investigate a legendary bottomless pit—lost in rumor and suspicion, mystery, even terror—under a full moon, probably arriving at about midnight! It doesn't get much better than this!"

"That's the way I see it, Darrell," I said. A true Minnesota boy could not , at this point, say that two men were freezing their butts off while out chasing moonbeams. Not me, anyway. I was committed.

We were already a mile down trail, and, I must admit, downhill. We had moved past the little church and were now threading our way down a very narrow dirt road that had forked off a wider dirt road a few hundred feet ago. We had descended, out of the moonlight, into deep shadow. He had admonished me to let the horses do the work—to let him do the navigating—to let the wolves do security in front and back and out to the sides of the riders, as was their routine.

"Spectacle," said Double-Dog Darrell. "Story. All your life you will be able to say you did this. Nobody will be able to take this away from you. Look up there at the ridge in that moonlight. Nobody gets to see that!" And the trail would turn and the moon would get a direct shot at us, and Double-Dog would give out a joyous cry.

In direct moonlight, I noticed on my saddle horn the initials D.D.D. Immediately, I wondered what Darrell knew about Milton's "Doctrine and Discipline in Divorce." I thought only English majors had to put up with that stuff. It was good for me, though. I decided then and there that I was not going to over-analyze this ride. D.D.D. meant Double-Dog Darrell, pure and simple.

Down and down, deeper and deeper into the valley we went. And it was as my captor had decreed: when Muffin trotted, Hacksaw trotted; when Muffin turned, Hacksaw turned; when Muffin tip-toed carefully along a narrow ledge with a goodly drop-off to one side, Hacksaw followed suit. I prayed that Muffin was sure-footed. I soon realized that if Muffin did a Double Lutz or a Triple Axel, Hacksaw was stuck with it. I prayed that Hacksaw was nimble and sure-footed.

The trotting was the worst. Real horsemen sit tight for it, but when you get on a horse once every twenty-five years, you bounce like a ping-pong ball, and there are a couple of little bones "down under" that serve as meat hammers on the inside while the saddle serves as butcher board on the outside. The rump "beef" between becomes hamburger and bone splinter, and the fun has just begun. I needed more Texas in me. The Minnesota part worked fine. I forgot all about the cold.

The trail hypnotizes, apparently: the rhythm of it, the monotony. And it was nighttime. Not too much detail. We did come upon a couple of branches thrown down across the trail by a recent ice storm, and there were some rock slides—all the normal , natural events. Much of the route was not a trail at all—just the only way through! There were no tracks that I could see. Double-Dog was navigating by landmarks he knew. A trail would have been obscured, in many areas, by fallen leaves. Still, I was more drowsy than excited.

Time became a factor. Evidently, my guide was wrong about doing the old Bottomless Pit bit at midnight. I had no real idea of where we were, but the pain in my nether parts indicated to me that we had done some traveling. I wondered if we would ever stop to rest, dismount, relax, build a fire, toast marshmallows, something! Then my rear went sorta numb, and I got to wondering about that. Had I damaged my spine and shut off the lower extremities? Was my body cutting off life support to all the fat now, or was it just that more blood was being sent to my cold areas? I looked at my watch when we came around a bend into the moonlight, and it was nearly 11 o'clock! I had missed Leno's monologue. I worried, quietly.

We crossed a stream then, and dropped even more steeply for a few minutes. Then we crossed the same stream, I think, a little wider this time, and slower. Muffin drank at both sites, and so Hacksaw did, too. I was glad for them. We slipped between two huge rocks, so tight a place that my toes scraped both sides. The horses had some fancy footwork to perform. I bumped my head on something above and pulled my neck in. Another low-hanging branch, brought lower by the ice storm. Then the trail straightened a little, and it hit a long, gently sloping stretch, heavily wooded left and right and over the top. It was dark. I could barely see the shapes of the wolves, and I couldn't imagine how Hacksaw was following Muffin.

I had the moment, then: the one I always have when I've been dragged into something that seems dumb, and I get outside of myself and ask, "All right, how in the hell did you get yourself into this mess?" And I defined my location: lost, cold, numb, out-of-control, probably in danger, yada yada yada. And the "If only" routine: If only I had not talked about the Bottomless Pit; if only I had shot Double-Dog as a burglar a year ago; if only I had stood up and refused—just stayed home in the warmth. And then, the "Next time" bit: Next time I'll tell them all to go to hell; Next time I'll just keep my skepticism to myself—hell, maybe there is a bottomless pit; Next time, when trouble comes in the front, I go out the back. All of that, but silently. I had a pact with myself about that.

❧

Eventually, we popped out onto a small flat area—a surprise to me—that just glowed in the moonlight. Dark cedars flanked it on all sides, and there was a huge cliff quite close in, and others all around, bordered at their bases by the cedar brush. From our angle, I could not see the top of the closest cliff wall. It looked absolutely black, for the moon was above it, throwing the cliff face into deep shadow. I was immediately certain that we would have to climb that cliff.

This clearing was a meadow-like spot. There was actual by-god grass. Muffin and Darrell stopped, and Darrell turned to me and said, "Get your right foot out of the stirrup. We're going to dismount—together. If I go first, Hacksaw will toss you into those cedars."

"Gotcha."

On three, we stepped down. Poetry in motion. I was on the ground, safe and sound at last. I patted Hacksaw and put my cold cheek against his warm neck. He bit my arm, but it didn't hurt much. I was on Earth again.

I looked around. We were down in a hole, and we were lucky to have light. I was lost, of course, but Darrell knew where he was, I was almost certain. He stepped over and disappeared into the cedars, I assumed to pee. The wolves formed a protective honor guard around him. I heard Double-Dog talking to himself, or maybe to the wolves. Nothing he did was amazing to me anymore, and I talked to everything myself: cats, dogs, coons, deer, anything that would sit still for it. Maybe he just talked at such introspective moments.

But we had been going down for a long time. Everything seemed to be up from where we were, and I could not imagine getting much deeper or much more remote from civilization, Scenic Byway Seven, security!. We had not seen an electric light in what seemed like hours. I had noticed my ears popping long ago and several layers up. I should be hearing a river, I reasoned: we were that low. I felt that we were below the level of the river, but that would have been impossible. I was more accustomed to sitting up top and looking down and over larger vistas from higher up. Here, visibility was limited, and I was disoriented. The moon cast such sharp shadows that wild shapes were everywhere, tempting the imagination, challenging reason. I wanted very much to whine, throw some sort of tantrum, stamp my foot. But Minnesota boys are supposed to be stoical and tough, and when they're old, they're supposed to shut up.

Little switchbacks in the trail, steep areas, the constant

angling down—all of it I had simply accepted. I asked no questions. I didn't want to talk to Darrell that much anyway, and give him smug satisfaction and stories to tell. But, so far, so good. I found cedar cover of my own.

"This isn't just a pit stop, you know," Darrell blurted, just as I was getting into my own personal pit stop. He was right at my elbow.

I flinched, but I did not leap into the air. I was busy. Marksmanship is important.

"Uh...it's impolite to point, too. Just thought I'd throw that in."

"Right," I said, finishing my pit stop. "Well, do we mount up and go on, or what?"

"No, we're there!" And he had that grin.

"We're there? Just like that? The Bottomless Pit?"

"Sure. I told you where we were going. It is nearly midnight, and I told you that we would be at the fabled Bottomless Pit at midnight, under a full moon, after half a horseback ride. That's where we are now."

&

One of the most annoying moments on PBS comes at the end of an expedition when an announcer like Stacey Keach or Alan Alda says, "Although the search did not turn up the dreamed-of sunken treasure, Doctor Fishwrinkle and the crew felt vindicated. Out of time and out of money, they had to return to port. But they had eliminated at least part of the mystery..." And I just knew that this was going to be like that. I sensed anticlimax. We were too deep into the earth for there to be a pit now! Jules Verne was nowhere in sight, and nothing else noteworthy was in sight either.

We tied our horses to the cedar brush well out from the base of the cliff, and Double-Dog Darrell yanked a bag of oats out from a pack on the back of Hacksaw (something I had wondered about). He did love those horses. Then I followed as Darrell walked toward the cliff. I was able to stand straight up after a few yards into the deep shadow. There was pain, but my back soon felt better, and my rear-end seemed grateful for the relief. My limp was stylish, young! I even put some swagger into my walk, I thought, but Double-Dog had to ask why I was staggering. I told him that swagger and stagger rhymed and that, as a poet, he should know that. He was not amused.

It got darker and darker, but soon we were close enough to see that some of the blackness at the base of the cliff was more cedar brush. We approached a heavy clump of the thick, dark, fragrant growth.

"You got your flashlight now?" asked Darrell.

"Yeah." I did a fast draw, and I flicked the button, and there was light.

"Let me show you," said Darrell, grabbing the light. He focused it on the dark mass before us, and through a break in the branches. It did no good. There was nothing behind the bushes except blackness. "There," said Darrell.

"There what?"

"What do you see?"

"Blackness. Is that it? Is that the pit?"

"That, my friend, is the bottom."

"The bottom."

"Of the so-called 'bottomless pit'."

"But the rules are, it has no bottom. I've heard about it all over the hills. You throw something down it, and it doesn't hit bottom. They throw bodies down it, remember? People disappear. Everybody says so. I have a right to bones: piles of bones! If this is the Bottomless Pit of legend, and if this is what I have been dragged out of the comfort of my stuffed chair and toasty living room to see, then, dammit, I demand a pit with no bottom."

He let me babble until I ran out of sardonic balderdash.

"You aren't paying attention. People don't come down here anymore. You can only see it from the air, and I don't know if you noticed it, but things were tight back there a ways. We are in a place nobody has visited in modern times. It's a box canyon. You can't drive here. You have to search for that passage. You can't hunt here, camp here, or canoe the river. Nobody knows about this place. And I found it because of the stories about the Bottomless Pit." He pointed the flashlight at the blackness again. "This isn't the pit; this is the bottom!"

"It's a cave, then," I said.

"Right above us is about 400 ft. of rock—layers, yes, but all rock. If you go to the top of this cliff and get back from its edge about fifty feet, that's where you find what these folks have been calling The Bottomless Pit—for generations! To get there, you drive back country dirt roads and walk a lot, but it's there, and some people actually go there. They throw things down the hole, and they don't hear it land. Bottomless Pit. Nobody's gonna go down to check it out. You know that."

"I thought there would be water."

"Nope. Just bat guano."

"Really?"

"Yeah. Pretty deep, pretty rank. Don't tell me you didn't suspect it. I think you told me once that you thought it was all a load of crap. Well, you were right. Come on." He started through the cedar brush into the black void.

"I don't like caves," I said, without the trace of a whine.

"Quit whining. Two days ago, I was up there on top with Cowboy John, and we threw something into the famous Bottomless Pit—for you! Now I am going to take you inside this slab of rock, and we are going to retrieve what I threw down the hole."

"What did you throw in?"

"A million dollars," he said with a mocking sneer.

"Yeah, right. Darrell, this is why some folks think you are a demon, a warlock, a sorcerer, a madman, and a nut. We are not here retrieving your million dollars. You never had a million dollars..."

"Joke. Just a joke," said Double-Dog. He was really being sane now. He had snap. He was with it. He was not stoned or spazzed or weirded out. He was just a little scary. "What I threw down the hole was a five-inch globe."

"Globe?"

"Yeah. A rendition of Mother Earth. A globe. Big Blue Marble. I'll bet it's here, right inside."

I looked for a way out, naturally; but I was trapped. Once, down under the Blue Ridge Mountains, I felt the weight of a whole mountain on top of me when I visited a cave, but I felt okay at Carlsbad, and I had been in caves in the Ozarks and in mines in the Rockies. Claustrophobia was not my problem. I just wanted to go home. I was through fooling around with the whole mess. I was tired, for God's sake—and I was retired! But the man had gone to a lot of trouble to put me through what he was sure was the adventure of my life. I was stuck, and enjoined from complaining.

According to Double-Dog Darrell, there were two levels of tourists in the hills. One level was those folks passing through, stopping up on the high ridges and looking at the gorgeous vistas and saying, "Ooooo" or "Ahhh," or grabbing a canoe and floating on the river. Another level, though, was folks who lived in the area and did not become involved with the earth, the rocks, the trees: observers, like me, who came to own, observe, and think—but not to be absorbed by the place. If you drowned in the river, Double-Dog liked you; if you just floated over it grinning in a canoe, you were a light-weight. Now, if I went inside this mountain to the very bottom of The Bottomless Pit, I would be acceptable: no longer a tourist. There had to be some sort of trial, or quest—an ordeal—a rite of passage.

"What the hell," I said, "I have come too far. Let's do it."

"Good decision. I just called your wife on my cell phone, and she figured you would go for it. I figured you would wimp out. I thought I was gonna have to use her on you."

I remember thinking, "Am I coward for capitulating, or would I be one for refusing?" So I chose to go in. (Lots of my choices are like that.)

We had to squat low, but we did not have to crawl on our

bellies. A few feet inside the little cave, we were able to stand up. I expected Darrell to light up a torch or a pine knot or something, but he pulled out a flashlight of his own. It was suddenly warmer, and I had the feeling of being indoors, and then of being under megatons of rock. I tossed the latter sensation aside, and started searching with my little beam of light.

The stench was terrible, but not as bad as I anticipated. A few more feet of just plain rock, and then Darrell stopped. "Look," he said, pointing his light at the ceiling. But there was no ceiling.

"Look at what?"

"At nothing. Just a hole. See there—just a big chimney! All the pit is, is a hole in the ground. It starts up there, and it ends down here."

"Have you been through it?"

"No. I have been to this spot, and I have been up there on top. But I don't think anybody has been through—in modern times, anyway."

"How do we know it goes all the way? How do we know there's not just a deep hole up there and a dark chimney down here?"

Double Dog lowered his light and we got a good look at what we were wading in. I had wondered about bat guano, and I was on the edge of nausea breathing it, and I wanted to go home. But I flashed my light around too. Just a lot of bat crap—probably deeper out further, right under the "chimney" opening. I had no desire to hang around and meet the bats themselves. The adventure was ending for me; the intrigue was not strong enough to keep me in that hole. I turned to leave, and my little light caught a flash of something blue over to the left.

"Wait a minute," I said.

"No, let's go," said Darrell. "You're skeptical. I guess we have to get up an expedition and drop through from the top."

"You do that, Double-Dog. But look over there—where I'm pointing my light."

We both stared. It was quite a moment, I have to say—even if Double-Dog staged it. "Uh...Houston, we've got a Big Blue Marble here," I narrated, "and you've got a couple of old guys about to have conniptions!"

"That's my globe," said Double-Dog Darrell somewhat excitedly. "I always told you that the world was in deep doo doo." Big grin again.

It was half-buried in the bat guano, in a little splash crater, really, and there were no tracks around it that I could see. We went outside the cave and got a long pole—dead but sturdy—and we went back in and raked that little globe toward us until we could reach it. Then we left that miserable hole forever—at least I did. (Darrell might go back, but that's his problem.)

"I will vouch for its authenticity," I vowed. "I can see how some might think this was a trick, but I believe you." I wanted to go home, but that has been mentioned.

"You don't have to vouch for anything," Darrell said. With a little blade, he opened the globe with a deft slash around its little Equator. By moonlight and flashlight, and any kind of light we could bring to the subject, the newspaper clipping inside the little five-inch globe told the story: a couple of green slashes above and below the banner of our hometown paper, then "Volume 84, Number 45, December 19, 2002." A picture of an elk, a picture of an inflatable Santa Claus. "Merry Christmas" and "JPs okay county budget..." In ink, "D.D.D." and "John Folger." I had wondered what Cowboy John's last name was. And, in a bolder ink, Wifey had signed her name!

"Looks like it made the trip," he said, "all the way through. Sorta the ultimate slam dunk!"

It was just twelve minutes into Sunday, December 22, and I was ready to mount up and hit the trail to hell out of there!

He could have had an accomplice in those bushes where I heard him talking, I suppose. Maybe it was Cowboy John, and not Wifey on a cell phone. I checked, and Darrell was in town at the Center chasing women on the Internet with their computer—on Thursday and Friday. Wifey and Madge Colstad swore they had substantive meetings with him in that time frame, too—setting me up! I know it took a lot of work to get the whole scam ready that Saturday, and I know that Muffin and Hacksaw could not do that trip twice in one day. Wifey admitted to signing the clipping. Maybe he smuggled the little globe in there under his coat and tossed it over there when our lights were focused elsewhere, but it was in deep and needed to be dug out. Or, somebody could have taken that globe out there and wedged it down into that foul crap, I suppose, and covered their tracks somehow, for some reason that escapes me. But, you know, I think it came down that shaft and plunged into that bat guano. I think we were at the bottom of the Bottomless Pit.

I intend to analyze it to death later, of course. Not now, for I have made promises not to. I need to find a loophole in a contract with myself. I am not sure the happening would take much scrutiny. A clever person might debunk the whole thing. Meanwhile, if someone asks me about The Bottomless Pit, I will tell him that it has a bottom, and that I have been there: at midnight, under a full moon, in the company of wolves—and at least one madman.

Chain Reaction

Pastor Cowell had been called to the ministry late in life. As a child he had not aspired to such an existence, and even as a young man he had been interested in other pursuits. But now, in his sermons at his small church, he was fond of pointing out that we ourselves do not always handle the timing or the planning in our lives. God had called him in His own time. (At least once, He waited until the guy was thirty.)

The parson's delivery was light-hearted, somewhat unfocused, but still "ministerial." He got the job done—with a smile, even when the job was labor-intensive. Above and beyond his duties as leader of his tiny flock, he had taken the reigns of the county's vital Pastor's Pantry, a food bank operation put together by the Association of Interdenominational Ministers (AIM), and he called the job a "blessing," even after two years. He was not tired, even though this blessing involved frequent trips across the mountains to another town to fetch small truckloads of food commodities purchased with local donations for distribution among our community's needy.

I knew about the pastor's work—had a good idea of the depth of his commitment—because it had been mentioned when he was introduced at the interfaith Thanksgiving service down in the village where he preached the guest sermon. Wifey and I were there, and I paid attention to his words, especially when he offered to "share the 'blessing' with any volunteer, anytime soon, Amen!" I also knew what it was like to step up and pinch hit for someone and end up tethered to home plate: to "fill in" temporarily in a vital role, and have to stay on indefinitely. It was an honor and a privilege, but an exhausting job. Still, Pastor Cowell had been called, he had answered, he had accepted, and he now considered his burden a blessing.

So I could imagine what was going on in the "heavily laden" little truck in front of us as Wifey and I returned from a last-minute Christmas shopping trip. There was traffic behind us, too, although all of us had been warned and should have known better. The weathermen in Springfield had called for snow, it is fair to say; but we had long since ceased believing their predictions. They could get the temperatures right, but precipitation in the mountains was another matter. This time they had said snow—possibly heavy in areas—and this time they were right. All of us had gone to Harrison anyway. Now it was coming down hard, and we were far from home on the mountain roads. Not good. Visibility was getting to be a problem.

I was glad to have Pastor Cowell in front of me. I knew his truck; everybody did. He had his lights on, and he was laying down fresh tracks to follow—good navigational aids for me. (Wifey was letting me drive because I had experienced driving in the snow from the old days in Nebraska and Iowa.) I could see the heavy load of food, and I knew that this was the Christmas batch, heading for our village to save Christmas for some lucky people. The Pastor was plugging away at his job, (accepting, accepting), and this time his burden/blessing was actually giving him traction! Still, I felt that it was unfair of God to tax this devout man further with weather complications. He drove cautiously. So did I, following closely.

Fact is, I had been identifying with Pastor Cowell in recent days, since his sermon. I was not of his flock, but I was there for the Thanksgiving service, and now I thought I knew him a little. He wanted to do more than he could do, I sensed—wanted to be more eloquent than he felt he was—wanted to say something or do something that would make things better—wanted to be used more wisely, perhaps. As an old worn-out teacher, I knew about dissatisfaction. He probably wondered if his teachings had hit home—if those entrusted to him "got it" when he delivered his messages. His message on behalf all of the ministers that night had to do with community: "One can do some, two can do more, three can do wonders, together we can move mountains." That sort of thing. Everybody nodded. We know these things, and we say these things, and we repeat them. But I just knew he had his doubts: not about The Word, or God, or his own sincerity, but about his effectiveness. He was probably praying about that as he drove. I could almost see his perpetual smile. I felt as if we were having some sort of intuitive conversation, he gripping his steering wheel, I mine.

Scenic Byway Seven is particularly snaky starting about five miles south of Harrison. It hits mountains and steep hairpin curves right away; then it dives down to the river and crosses a bridge, and then it climbs up over more mountains and then worms its way down again into Jasper. Often there's a rock face on one side and a goodly drop-off on the other, slippery when wet, potentially terrifying in snow, dicey even on a good day. In bad weather, it is good to have a country preacher leading the way! I insist.

We crossed the Buffalo River on the bridge that was now one-way, and we sped-up a little for the climb up out of the valley. I noticed that there were no on-coming tracks, only the pastor's tracks. Visibility allowed that much. But it meant that nobody was coming toward us: that trouble lay ahead. Yeah. It was good to have the pastor in front of me—with his connections.

"Put in a good word for all of us, Rev," I grunted in my cynical way, squinting at my windshield.

There was still some daylight, or the heavy snowfall would already have stopped us—stopped us cold—miles back. Headlights and heavy snow don't work well together. The forest above and below and all around us was filling up with beautiful snow, but I was forced to concentrate on the road and not wish that I could draw, not wish that I had a camera along, not wish I could stop and watch as the peace settled in. I hung onto the wheel and followed the preacher.

～

A few hundred yards south of the Buffalo River bridge, uphill and around a couple of mild curves, and just as I became convinced that we were doing well, Pastor Cowell slammed his little truckload of food into a snow bank, and it was time for everybody to pray.

In a sheltered area on the climb up from the bridge, a deposit of new snow, whipped into the form of a low, thick wall, reached completely across the road, and we were all abruptly stopped: Pastor Cowell, Wifey and I, and behind us, off into the storm and downhill around the bend, a chain of several others, God only knew how many. The snow seemed to fall even harder, and what visibility there was faded considerably. Ahead, I could see that the pastor had led this flock into a considerable pile of trouble.

～

"Oh boy," I muttered, shifting my old Dodge into Park. I had a moment to conjure up a whole nightmare of snow and cold and misery and emergency flares and blankets and shivering and teeth-chattering and fresh-frozen melodrama. I'm good at that. I could see it all. I felt sorry for the others. Me? I'm a Minnesota boy. Not to worry.

I only remember a few specific things that were said during the rest of the episode. It became a remarkably vocal, but wordless exercise. Wifey said, "You're on," and, as I reluctantly slipped out into the elements, pulling on my gloves, she slipped into the driver's seat. I probably said, "Yes, Dear," or something equally poignant and prompt.

I moved forward to check out the pastor, and about the time I saw his smile—snow hitting him in the face, his breath visible as puffs of steam, his cold teeth reflecting headlights—I was nudged from behind. I noticed the pastor looking at me, through me, and past me, smiling. At my elbow was one man, and eight more were coming up the road through the storm—eight that I could see—like links in a chain. In my own little melodrama, the minister made eye contact with me and confirmed that we had talked this whole thing over.

Nobody spoke much more than a greeting. We knew each other. These were local men, young and old, rich and poor, common and un. The tourists were gone for the winter, and this was our show. Everybody knew what to do and why to do it. "One can do some, two can do more, three can do wonders, together we can move mountains." We were together.

More or less silently, certainly at first, we shoved the pastor's truck uphill and through the snow bank as he drove. When free, he pulled ahead and parked in the truck pull-off that is located at that point on the highway, and he returned— just in time for his action to teach the rest of us. It's not just aboug getting through, it's about going back for the others. Wifey parked by the pastor's little truck after we all pushed my old Dodge through the barrier: a good ten of us. Then she shut the car off and joined the party.

Yeah, Wifey had to get out and push. It was what was being done, and she could not merely watch! Nobody could. Other women joined us soon. We stayed and helped the pastor and the gang push five or six more cars through, and together we kicked and scraped and pounded that snow bank down. Then it got to be fun as more cars arrived: all that grunting and laughing, then cheering as each vehicle reached at least temporary freedom. Headlights, taillights, spotlights, emergency flashers, signal lights—a merry, festive display! There were even bright new shovels! And the snow became beautiful—Christmas snow—a burden and a blessing. Soon, the cars could almost make it without help.

Uphill just a couple of sharp turns, a state road maintainer, roaring and flashing and looking all orange and fearsome and Christmassy, was soon detected heading in our direction in its self-generated cloud, clearing the highway of further trouble, at least temporarily. We huddled in the truck pull-out, cheering as the beast edged by, and then the whole caravan mounted up and got back on the road. Someone else took the lead, but Wifey and I waited and followed the pastor and his little truck, burdened with a blessing, and heading for home.

We learn all the time, and we teach all the time: together. A gesture, a smile, a sermon, a mumbling of worn-out words, perhaps, can get us through the rough spots. It takes so little. We will seize upon any lame excuse to be decent, to help each other muddle through, to be part of something bigger than we are, to count for something, to celebrate, to give back. And every now and then someone sets off a chain reaction.